D1596798

Making America Green and Safe

Making America Green and Safe:

A History of Sustainable Development and Climate Change

By

Alan D. Hecht

Cambridge
Scholars
Publishing

Making America Green and Safe:
A History of Sustainable Development and Climate Change

By Alan D. Hecht

This book first published 2018

Cambridge Scholars Publishing

Lady Stephenson Library, Newcastle upon Tyne, NE6 2PA, UK

British Library Cataloguing in Publication Data
A catalogue record for this book is available from the British Library

ISBN (10): 1-5275-1378-5
ISBN (13): 978-1-5275-1378-5

CONTENTS

Past Present and Future

AN ENVIRONMENTAL HISTORY DEDICATED TO THE CAREER CIVIL SERVICE

This book aims to give you both a historical perspective and an insider's view of the evolution of science and policy actions on climate change and steps toward building a resilient and sustainable society especially at the Environmental Protection Agency (EPA).

From a government perspective, I have found that achieving progress on these issues has not been easy. In the case of climate change, we have lost the ability to prevent climate change but instead must now adapt to it. Historians have long recognized that the American political system is not efficient or effective in organizing change, and that working in this environment, especially across administrations, is never easy and often frustrating. Civil servants often confront intense anti-government fervor and must remain innovative in providing the knowledge and energy essential for government operations.

For these reasons, I dedicate this book to all members of the federal workforce. I especially recognize and applaud the staff at the EPA who are devoted to protecting human health and the environment and who have dealt with intense and unjustified political attacks. They deserve the dedication of this book.

Throughout the book I also acknowledge and reference the work of many colleagues and innovative thinkers who have advanced the work on sustainability and climate change. These scientists and policy-makers have helped Make America Green and Safe.

About the Author

I have worked in government for over 42 years. My early career focused on climate change research, first as a teacher and researcher, then as a policy maker. While I was teaching geology from 1970 to 1976 at West Georgia College (now West Georgia University), a colleague in the History Department, Newt Gingrich and I undertook one of the earliest environmental study programs in Georgia. I came to Washington in 1976 and he came in 1978.

From 1976 to 1982, I worked at the National Science Foundation (NSF) as the first director of the Climate Dynamics Program with responsibility for funding research in atmospheric sciences, climate modeling, paleoclimatology, and the social impacts of climate change.

At NSF, I met some of the smartest people in science. Many grantees that I funded won all the prestigious awards in their fields, including the Nobel Prize. I also had the privilege of starting the careers of many productive and creative earth scientists. There were painful moments as well. Denying support to a young scientist vying for tenure is painful. I had more than one tearful and emotional conversation with young scientists about their work, and their future activities. On another occasion, I found it necessary to end the support to a scientist, who after a long and productive career was no longer competitive. It was uncomfortable for me as a young man in his thirties to tell a respected scientist in his seventies that, in effect, "you've had it." NSF taught me that life in government is more than just shuffling paper, but was in effect a mixture of strategic planning, good management and behavior science.

In 1982, I moved to the National Oceanic and Atmospheric Administration (NOAA) at the Department of Commerce to become the Director of the National Climate Program Office (NCPO). In this position from 1982 to 1989, I led 15 federal agencies in developing US policy on climate research, negotiated the first climate change agreement, and proposed and helped to create the Intergovernmental Panel on Climate Change (IPCC).

The IPCC is an international science assessment body that was instrumental in fostering US government consensus on the need for an international treaty to reduce the impact of human-created climate change. Today, the US Global Change Research Program has replaced the NCPO.

While working at the NCPO, I learned another important lesson of life in Washington. When I first became the NCPO Director, I saw my role largely as a communicator and bridge-builder between the many federal agencies involved in climate change. In time, I saw my job differently, realizing that the role of a *coordinator* is more than a passive communicator among agencies, but rather an aggressive *synthesizer* of ideas. The coordinator's job is to make the whole more than the sum of its parts. Like some biologists, the coordinator must see the whole organism, and understand how each part interacts with the other. It does not take long to learn that each agency has their own individual traits, which dictate their behavior, but the coordinator must see the government function in an integrated manner. This lesson has guided me in everything I have done, especially in my work at EPA.

In 1989, William K. (Bill) Reilly, the newly appointed Administrator of the US Environmental Protection Agency (EPA) recognized that environmental problems are part of a much larger picture of trade policy and economic and social development. It was Administrator Reilly who hired me to help develop EPA's international program. As the Principal Deputy Assistant Administrator for the Office of International Activities, I expanded EPA's international programs to forge new directions for the agency in international policy and research, trade and the environment, capacity development, export promotion, environment and national security, and sustainable development.

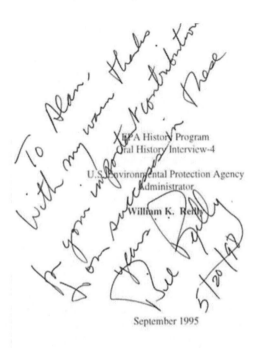

EPA History Program
Oral History Interview-4

U.S. Environmental Protection Agency
Administrator

William K. Reilly

September 1995

Working with Bill Reilly was a great honor and I respect his note to me in 1995 saying "with warm thanks for your important contributions for our success in these years."

During the Clinton Administration, I led EPA's negotiating team for the environmental side agreement to the North American Free Trade Agreement (NAFTA) and participated in negotiating for and setting up the North American Development Bank, the NAFTA-created Commission on Environmental Cooperation, and the US-Mexico Border Program. For over five years, I traveled extensively across the US-Mexico border and came to appreciate the hard work of the career workforce on the border.

A career civil servant doing his job on the US-Mexico border—photograph by Alan Hecht

During the administration of George W. Bush from 2001 to 2003, I was on detail from EPA to the National Security Council (NSC) and the Council on Environmental Quality (CEQ). I started my White House assignment one month after the terrorist attacks of September 11, 2001. In the White House, I helped coordinate preparations for the 2002 World Summit on Sustainable Development in Johannesburg.

After returning to EPA in 2003, I led the agency's research activities on sustainability. Making sustainability an EPA goal has been a difficult road to travel. It is, however, something that is essential to ensure a sound and stable national economy over the coming decades. The first chapters of this book capture EPA's long history making sustainability an agency-wide goal.

Over my 40 years in government and despite the drawbacks of working in Washington and my frustration with management, I remained in public service, believing I could do something good for society. I have had many successes in improving the global environment, developing new environmental policies, launching new programs, enhancing national security, negotiating agreements, and training young people and seeing their careers develop. I was also honored in 1999 to get the President's Rank Award that honors high-performing senior career employees for "sustained extraordinary accomplishment."

In sum, I am indebted to many friends and colleagues who have both helped guide and rescue me over my long career. I am also grateful to many colleagues who have reviewed and helped to edit these chapters. These include Gordon Binder, Joseph Fiksel, Mike McCracken and Aaron Ferster who did a final editing of the book. Throughout the book I have included many photographs and cartoons downloaded from Google's images. Thank you Google.

PREFACE

WILLIAM K. REILLY
EPA ADMINISTRATOR 1989-2003

With this book, a grand summary of past, current, and future actions by business and government to address our environmental challenges, Alan Hecht has made a significant contribution. The world over, we confront challenges with serious consequences for our health, the environment, and the natural resources on which we depend, our economy and our quality of life included.

Topping the list is climate change, which increasingly is seen as affecting communities and natural resources across the globe. The demand for resources as population grows and more people achieve economic security is having profound impacts on water, on energy, on forests, soils, and other land uses, on estuaries and marine life, and more.

As other countries must do, we, too, as a nation must find ways to bolster community resiliency and plan for a sustainable future. Our children, our grandchildren, future generations of Americans deserve nothing less.

I met Alan Hecht during my tenure as EPA Administrator. We put a priority on integrating environmental protection and the economy, strengthening the role of science at EPA, and recognizing the centrality of place-based approaches to improving the environment. We also played a key role in advancing international cooperation, including on climate change.

It was this issue, the brewing concern over climate change that prompted my invitation to Alan to join the EPA team in our newly elevated Office of International Activities. In 1989, he was leading the National Climate Program Office and was a key player coordinating activities across many federal agencies. Late in my tenure, he proved especially helpful as I led the US delegation to the Earth Summit in Rio de Janeiro in June 1992. His critical climate research had helped pave the way for a treaty on climate change, which was unveiled at the Summit.

Alan also played a critical role with the Soviet Union in dealing with the disposal of nuclear waste. And after I left EPA, he became the chief negotiator for a critically needed environmental side agreement to support the passage of NAFTA, including extensive bilateral cooperation with Mexico to protect the border area. After his time in EPA's international office, he went to the White House for 2 years, returning to EPA to lead the Agency's endeavors on sustainable development.

In this book, Alan writes about the history of science and policy actions on climate change and on steps to advance sustainable development. The concluding chapter on megatrends underscores why progress on these issues is so essential.

The book is timely considering the pressures now on EPA. Now more than ever business and government must work together to achieve a resilient and sustainable society. Now more than ever, we must take actions to reduce the ongoing impacts of climate change which are a threat to our economic future.

Alan Hecht deserves great credit for his more than 40 years in government and his dedication to the career civil service. He clearly and cogently makes the case that EPA has the experience, knowledge, resources, and commitment to lead in research and technological applications supporting wise decisions and responsible stewardship.

A central theme of this book is that understanding history is critical in planning future activities. Read the book and ask yourself, are we on the right track? Are we adequately protecting public health and the environment for future generations, as well as for our own? Are we preparing, as we should, for what's coming? Are we ensuring that the agencies and institutions we rely on to set the course remain viable and productive? The answers will say a lot about the world future generations will inherit.

Bill Reilly and Alan Hecht at EPA

OFTEN CITED ACRONYMS

CEQ: Council on Environmental Quality
CIA: Central Intelligence Agency
CO2: Carbon Dioxide
CSD: Commission on Sustainable Development
EPA: Environmental Protection Agency
GHS: Greenhouse gases
IPCC: Intergovernmental Panel on Climate Change
ICSU: International Council for Science
NAS: National Academy of Sciences
NCPO: National Climate Program Office
NEPA: National Environmental Protection Act
NIC: National Intelligence Council
NOAA: National Oceanic and Atmospheric Administration
NSC: National Security Council
NSF: National Science Foundation
ORD: Office of Research and Development
PCSD: Presidential Council on Sustainable Development
UNCED: The United Nations Conference on Environment and
    Development
UNEP: The United Nations Environmental Program
UNFCCC: The United Nations Framework Convention on Climate
    Change
USGCRP: United States Global Change Research Program
WBCSD: World Business Council for Sustainable Development
WCC: World Climate Conference
WCRP: World Climate Research Program
WMO: World Meteorological Organization
WSSD: World Summit on Sustainable Development

INTRODUCTION

HISTORY MATTERS AND WHAT IS SUSTAINABILITY?

"Once you stop learning, you start dying"
—Albert Einstein

Past, Present, Future: History Matters

I strongly believe that understanding history is a critical part of future planning. As noted by George Santayana (1863-1952) "Those who do not remember the past are condemned to repeat it."

Hence this book explores the history of steps toward achieving sustainable development and dealing with climate change. The goal is to enhance insights about how best to deal with future needs.

Like Hillary Clinton, I thought I'd title my book "What Happened." Except what happened in this book is real!

It reflects my history in the federal government and the global work to advance sustainable development and respond to climate change. While progress has been made, the future is not clear, given current politics, especially in the context of EPA.

In dealing with the politics of today and the problems at EPA, I acknowledge the great quote from David Barry (March 22, 1999)

> We live in troubled times, but I feel good about myself, about my homeland and about all nations, and yes, about the future of humanity. And I will tell you why; I am on painkillers.

Painkillers are not what we want for the future. Instead we must take actions to move toward a resilient and sustainable world by dealing with a great many stressors on society, not the least of which is climate change.

The first four chapters trace the history of the concept of sustainability and sustainable development beginning with the creation of the National Environmental Policy Act (NEPA) and EPA in 1970, and the first earth summit in Stockholm in 1972. Chapter 4 is an extensive history of the evolution of sustainability at EPA, moving the Agency from its classic role as a regulator and policeman to an effective communicator and science leader.

The second set of chapters (5-7), beginning with an extensive chronology of events over the past 50 years, deals with the history of the science and policy debate on climate change. The basic message here is that climate change is real! The diagram below is from the *New York Times*, January 21, 2018.

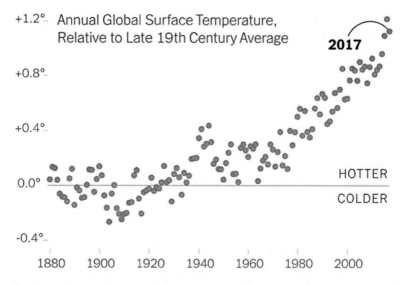

The last chapter is a crucial assessment of current challenges, called megatrends which we must face today to keep America green and safe.

The key goal of my book is to enhance academic and public understanding of the urgency and need for achieving sustainability and the decades-long debate on climate change policy and associated risks. Lessons learned about the past, enhance our opportunity to protect the future.

As you read all that follows consider answering these questions:

Q: In the world today, how do we best deal with the complex interaction of environmental, social and economic problems?

Q: How do we ensure strong economic growth while protecting the environment?

Q: What factors are currently limiting the business world in terms of their sustained operations?

Q: What is the best model for business-government collaboration in the decades ahead?

Q: Why do some conservatives object to the concept of "sustainability" or a "green environment"? And

Q: Why do some extremists deny the reality of climate change?

No test at the end. But history may help you plan the next steps for the future.

Let's begin with an understanding of what is sustainability.

What is Sustainability and Sustainable Development?

The idea of sustainability is to ensure growth and prosperity in a healthy environment that does not impede future development. In a classic definition, a sustainable society is "one that can persist over generations; one that is far seeing enough, flexible enough and wise enough not to undermine its physical or its social system of support."[1]

---

[1] Meadows, D. H., D. L. Meadows and J. Randers, 1992, *Beyond the Limits*. White River Junction, VTL Chelsea Green Publications.

Sustainability reflects the necessary and successful integration and advancement of economic growth, environmental protection, and social well-being. The often quoted three pillars of sustainability are:

1. Economic prosperity driven by production, manufacturing, trade and recycling.
2. Environmental protection of air, water, soils, mineral resources and biota.
3. Social justice including protecting human health and social equality.

In practice, sustainability is both a **goal** and a **process** for effective resource production and management. The goal is to maximize economic return, while protecting the environment and ensuring social well-being. To accomplish this requires integrated thinking since actions on one pillar strongly impact the others. It also requires moving beyond just risk reduction and single medium pollution control.

This point was emphasized in a report from the National Academy of Sciences (NAS) to EPA in 2011 saying: "Current approaches aimed at decreasing existing risks, however successful, are not capable of avoiding the complex problems in the United States and globally that threaten the planet's critical natural resources and that put current and future human generations at risk."[2]

---

[2] NAS, 2011, "Sustainability and the US," EPA.

For your information, throughout this book I will refer to the NAS, and cite their many reports to Congress and Federal Agencies. The NAS was created by President Lincoln in 1863 and is a nonpartisan group of scientists who serve society by addressing the conflicts over critical issues such as climate change and by identifying potential new threats to society.

NAS was charged with "providing independent, objective advice to the nation on matters related to science and technology. ... to provide scientific advice to the government 'whenever called upon' by any government department." NAS Reports are unbiased, nonpolitical and scholarly.

The challenge today both for government and business is to get ready for the future. For the business world, sustainability goes beyond "business as usual" and is based on innovation in the design, production and reuse of products. As my colleagues David Lubin and Dan Esty (2010) noted, businesses must "do things in new ways and do new things in new ways."[3]

And for government, advancing sustainability is an essential element of a growing economy. As noted (in 1987) by the first administrator of the EPA William Ruckelshaus

> "Sustainable development not only conserves resources (including land), but also reduces long-term costs associated with maintaining infrastructure and supplying essential services. Efficient development also maximizes the availability of human resources to businesses. That translates into long-term economic viability that is less subject to the volatility associated with fluctuating energy and raw material prices."

Urgency of Sustainability Today

In the world today, more than at any time in the past, achieving sustainability and sustainable development is critical in dealing with a suite of megatrends impacting our lives. These are discussed in detail in the last chapter. They include population growth, especially in cities and dealing with the impacts of climate change.

The many pressures impacting government and business and the need to deal with them in an integrated manner were made abundantly clear in a 2017 Report on "Global Trends" from the National Intelligence Council (NIC).

---

[3] David Lubin and Dan Esty, "The Sustainability Imperative," *Harvard Business Review* 2010.

NIC, which advises the Central Intelligence Agency, conducts studies on assessing existing pressures and projected impacts on global society.

In this study on "Global Trends," they noted that: "The Earth's systems are undergoing natural and human-induced stresses **outpacing national and international environmental protection efforts.**"

Hence, we need to be more efficient and effective in managing our resources.

The NIC Report also said:

> "Institutions **overseeing single sectors will increasingly struggle to address the complex interdependencies** of water, food, energy, land, health, infrastructure, and labor."

The interdependencies among food, energy, water and land use are now a common theme in both business and government. It is often called the "nexus of food, energy and water." This reflects the intricate links between food, energy, land, and water management where water supply is influenced by demands from the energy and food sectors; food production requires both water and energy; and energy requires water for a large fraction of its production and delivery.

Projected growth in populations will make this nexus even more of a priority in that it is estimated that with a population of 8.3 billion people by 2030, society will need 50% more energy, 40% more water, and 35% more food.

Hence integrated or systems thinking is a critical factor in achieving a sustainable society and action on the 3 pillars of sustainability must be advanced by business and government to generate a green and safe society. It is here that advances in science and technology and the development of what are called decision-support tools can make a big difference in advancing sustainability. More on this is in Chapter 4.

Resilience and Sustainability

A key element of sustainability today is an understanding of "resilience" which is the ability of systems to anticipate, prepare for, and adapt to changing conditions and withstand, respond to, and recover rapidly from disruptions. While sustainability focuses on improving long-term conditions, resilience focuses on overcoming urgent short-term challenges that may hinder progress toward long-term goals.

Resilience is more urgent today than ever because of the impacts of climate change and rising costs in dealing with extreme weather events. Resilience is thus a critical part of a safe and sustainable future. Again, more on this is in Chapter 4.

Over time, how has the concept of sustainability and resilience evolved and how has EPA made it part of its classic regulatory role? And given the politics of today, especially related to EPA, how can we create a green and safe society?

Political Attachment on Sustainability

One of my goals in this book is to enhance public understanding of what is sustainability, since it is often attacked politically. Some harsh critics look at sustainability, especially as advanced by environmental and social advocates as a push toward more regulation and intrusion on social rights. This is far from the reality.

Yet, in his book, *Green Hell*, Steve Milloy argued, "And what about the most ubiquitous of green terms, sustainable development? What does it mean? Does it mean we can't use a natural resource unless there is an endless supply of it? Does it mean we can't use a resource if getting at it or using it alters the environment, however trivially or transiently, in some way or shape? For the greens, the answer to these questions is yes."

See: http://www.simonandschuster.com/books/Green-Hell/Steven-Milloy/ 9781596985858)

Sustainability is far from a "green hell" in which environmentalists plan to control your life.

It is instead a critical next step to advance economic growth, environmental protection and social well-being. The potential economic value of sustainability is not merely to decrease environmental risks but to optimize the social and economic benefits of environmental protection.

The Next Decades

By anticipating and responding to future challenges, we can disprove Benjamin Franklin's classic adage, "It is not until the well runs dry that we know the worth of water."

In looking ahead, my colleague Joseph Fiksel and I have advanced 8 critical steps for advancing sustainability:

1. *Take the long view: Sustainability requires long-term thinking, not only in natural resource management and urban development, but also in corporate strategic planning.*
2. *Understand the system dynamics:* Traditional industrial and engineering systems were not created with a systems view, and may therefore be vulnerable to unexpected disruptions, such as natural disasters, industrial accidents, sabotage, or terrorism. By understanding system vulnerabilities and leverage points, we can develop cost-effective and resilient management strategies.
3. *Define sustainability goals:* President Kennedy set a goal for the United States to land on the moon. This goal was achieved because it was fully supported with the needed resources and policies. Making sustainable development an explicit policy goal at all levels of government, as well as the private sector, can send a clear message about the need for breakthrough innovation and creative regulatory and compliance approaches that serve the collective interests of the public, business, and government.
4. *Use effective tools:* Science and technology are key underlying contributors, along with innovative environmental and economic policies. A growing body of economic and environmental assessment tools is available to support planners and decision-makers at all levels of government and industry.
5. *Find the right collaborators:* Collaboration and partnerships among stakeholders are crucial to achieving solutions that are less polarized, more economically viable, and focused on balancing short- and long-term goals. Collaboration has begun among government, industrial, and non-governmental organizations, and has already yielded many sustainable innovations.
6. *Lead by example:* The profound changes needed to achieve sustainability will require confidence and bold leadership. The most persuasive approach for overcoming uncertainty and hesitation is leading by example—demonstrating that these changes are both realistic and beneficial.

7. ***Measure and track progress:*** Indicators can help managers and policy makers anticipate and assess key trends, provide early warning of potential disruptions, quantify progress toward sustainability goals, and support decision-making about complex trade-offs.

8. ***Learn and adapt:*** The path to sustainability cannot be planned precisely due to the enormous complexity and uncertainty inherent in global political, economic, social, and natural systems. We must be prepared to learn from experience, rethink our assumptions, and continuously adapt to change. Taking a resilient approach in the short-term will enable sustainability in the long-term.

For our successful future, all sectors of society will need to work together to advance these principles which are essential to assuring continued American prosperity and competitiveness. The public must come to understand that sustainability provides both the vision and the approach to achieve outcomes that enhance the economy and protect health and the environment.

The history of steps toward achieving sustainability begins in the early days of pollution control, in the 1960s and 1970s. On the international scene, four major conferences, in 1972, 1992, 2002 and 2012, have advanced the concepts of sustainability. On the domestic front, the goal of sustainability has been advanced by both government and business. For EPA, it has been a major step forward in aligning problems and advancing science to deal with present and future problems.

Step 1 begins now.

DEALING WITH SUSTAINABLE DEVELOPMENT

Chapter One

Creation of NEPA, EPA and the 1972 Stockholm Earth Summit

From: www.pophistorydig.com.

My historic review begins with the 1960s and 1970s when many events affecting the environment and human health attracted public attention. This was a time of serious air pollution and water contamination. A 1969 oil slick fire in the Cuyahoga River in Ohio drew national attention to environmental problems in the Great Lakes region and elsewhere in the country.

What was going on in the 1960s and 1970s was recently mentioned in an interview in 2015 with EPA's first Administrator, William Ruckelshaus who in 2015 was awarded the President's Medal of Freedom.

He said that in the 1960s we "had all kinds of evidence flashing across television screens every morning or every evening about rivers catching on fire, smog alerts, badly polluted waters and air all over the country. And people were reacting to that and demanding action. And they saw the action was primarily at the state level and so they were strongly encouraging the federal government to take a more major role."

Some more attention to the pollution of the 1970s came from Robert Boyle, who in an article in *Sports Illustrated* (October 1970) entitled "Poison Roams Our Coastal Seas," identified a number of chemical contaminants in game fish from the Atlantic, the Gulf of Mexico, and Pacific coasts and in striped bass from the Hudson River.

A year later, he wrote to the chief of the Bureau of New York Fisheries, telling him of the high levels of PCBs in striped bass in the Hudson and urging him to warn anglers not to eat these fish. Then in a 1976 article, Boyle wrote about "poisoned fish and troubled waters" affecting dozens of American waterways.

All the events of the 1960s and 1970s led to bipartisan action to protect human health and the environment. In the world today, the concept of "bipartisan" may not be fully understood.

What Congress did was create the historic National Environmental Policy Act (NEPA) which was one of the first laws ever written that established a broad national framework for protecting the environment. President Nixon signed it on January 1, 1970.

NEPA's basic policy, still functioning today, is to ensure that all branches of government consider the environmental impacts of any major federal action that significantly affects the environment. One critical element of NEPA was the establishment of the President's Council on Environmental Quality (CEQ) which over time has produced critical reports for the President on sustainability, climate change and other critical issues.

While NEPA established the CEQ, it did not deal with the growing problem of air and water pollution. To address these issues, President Nixon turned to his Advisory Council on Executive Organization chaired by Roy L. Ash (the Ash Council). They in turn began to consider reorganizing existing agencies and programs into what would become the EPA.

Ultimately, they recommended the integration of anti-pollution programs from five other federal departments into one new agency. Accepting this idea, President Nixon created the EPA by executive order in December 1970. Once the EPA was created, Congress followed up with a series of critical legislations to restrict pollution from impacting human health.

From its creation in December 1970, the EPA began its role in controlling pollution and would soon become what Phillip Shabecoff called "the federal government's watchdog, police officer, and chief weapon against all forms of pollution."[4] Addressing the obvious environmental problems of the 1970s while being well received by many was also the beginning of a business-government conflict which remains today especially in dealing with climate change.

In NEPA, though the term was not used, the concept of sustainability was captured by establishing a national goal of creating and maintaining "conditions under which humans and nature can exist in productive harmony, and fulfill the social, economic and other requirements of *present and future generations of Americans* [emphasis added]."

This goal in 1970 is a remarkable precursor to the definition of sustainable development that would come in the 1987 UN-sponsored report (Our Common Future) "Sustainable development is development that meets the needs of the present without compromising the ability of future generations to meet their own needs."

NEPA also laid out the following critical goals. Given the craziness of politics today, ask yourself how well government is addressing these issues.

- Long-term Planning: "fulfill the responsibilities of each generation as a trustee of the environment for succeeding generations;"
- Equity: "assure for all Americans safe, healthful, productive, and esthetically and culturally pleasing surroundings;"
- Widespread Prosperity: "achieve a balance between population and resource use that will permit high standards of living and a wide sharing of life's amenities;"

---

[4] Phillip Shabecoff, *A Fierce Green Fire: The American Environmental Movement*, New York, Hill & Wang, 1993, 122.

- Resource Management: "enhance the quality of renewable resources and approach the maximum attainable recycling of depletable resources."

Even though it is 1970, NEPA was also very far reaching in promoting "environmental justice" by requiring federal agencies to include communities of color and low-income communities in their NEPA-mandated environmental analyses.

First International Earth Summit in Stockholm 1972

Following actions on NEPA and the creation of the EPA, there was also growing international attention on environmental issues and a clear divide between developed and developing countries. In 1967, Börje Billner, Sweden's Deputy Permanent Representative to the UN, proposed to the General Assembly that a conference be held to "facilitate co-ordination and to focus the interest of member countries on the extremely complex problems related to the human environment."

The UN accepted this proposal and organized in 1972 the first United Nations Conference on the Human Environment subtitled "Only One Earth." For the first time, environmental issues commanded attention at a high level of international governance. Three World Conferences would follow in 1992, 2002 and 2012.

My late colleague, Maurice Strong of Canada played a key role in organizing this conference in Stockholm and subsequently the 1992 Earth Summit in Rio. His leadership in 1972 was crucial in beginning to address a host of emerging threats to the natural environment and in advancing the crucial role of the United Nations. After the 1972 Summit, Strong served as the first Executive Director of the United Nations Environment Program (UNEP).

He died at the age of 86 in November 2015. I wrote a blog honoring him and noted that no one deserved more credit than him for advancing the goals of sustainability. The blog is available at https://blog.epa.gov/blog/tag/maurice-strong/. Even delegates at the Paris climate conference in 2015 paid tribute to his vision and accomplishments.

In planning the Stockholm Conference, Strong was clever enough to commission a study led by Barbara Ward and Rene Dubos (Only One Earth) that underscored the growing industrial stressors on the environment and the depletion of natural resources. Their Report, entitled "*Only One Earth*," with input from 58 countries made it clear that "man must accept responsibility for the stewardship of the earth."

This was the first major Report to emphasize the potential for the depletion of natural resources and to project potential impacts due to population increase, projecting an increase to 7 billion people by the year 2000. Concurrent with their projected increase in population growth by 2000, "urban inhabitants, nearly three and a half billion (in 1970) will outstrip rural people for the first time."

Only One Earth made it clear that the growing footprint of man on the environment needed better management. That was 1972, and many studies that followed made the same point.

At the Conference, the US was represented by the late Russell Train (1920-2012) who was head of the CEQ and would later be an Administrator for EPA. In remarks to the Conference, he telegraphed to the world one overriding issue for sustainable development. He said that "the US had learned that economic development at the expense of the environment imposes heavy costs to health and in the quality of life generally—costs that could be minimized by forethought and planning."

Train's speech laid the foundation for a broader discussion of sustainability that would come years later. While still a contentious issue today among some conservatives it is now apparent to business and government that economic growth and environmental protection can be mutually supportive.

The above quote and his other thoughts on the conference were nicely summarized in his biography "Politics, Pollution and Pandas: An Environmental Memoir" (2003). He further noted that "no longer should there be any qualitative differences between the goals of the economist and those of the ecologists."

The Stockholm Conference was affected by the politics of the 1970s. For example, the Soviet Union and other Warsaw Pact nations boycotted it because of the lack of inclusion of East Germany, which was not allowed to participate as it was not a full member of the UN.

The Conference also had divisions between developed and developing countries. The Chinese delegation was hostile to the United States and issued a memorandum condemning United States policies around the world.

Despite the above, the Stockholm Conference was successful and in effect started to put political attention on environment issues. Maurice Strong noted that the Conference "marked the first time that the nations of the world collectively acknowledged that something had gone wrong with the way in which man had been managing . . . his relationship with the natural world on which his own survival depends."

The meeting did end with a Declaration containing 26 principles concerning the environment and development, many of which are key elements of actions needed for advancing a sustainable society.

These include:

2. Natural resources must be safeguarded;
3. The Earth's capacity to produce renewable resources must be maintained;
5. Non-renewable resources must be shared and not exhausted;
6. Pollution must not exceed the environment's capacity to clean itself;
8. Development is needed to improve the environment;
11. Environment policy must not hamper development;
13. Integrated development planning is needed;
14. Rational planning should resolve conflicts between the environment and development;
15. Human settlements must be planned to eliminate environmental problems;
18. Science and technology must be used to improve the environment;
19. Environmental education is essential;
20. Environmental research must be promoted, particularly in developing countries;
24. There must be cooperation on international issues.

Following the Stockholm Conference, the UN General Assembly in the fall of 1972 met to discuss, among other things a new institutional and financial framework for protecting the environment. Actions at the UN in NY, under the influence of Maurice Strong led to the creation of the United Nations Environmental Program (UNEP) for which he was its first Director.

The Stockholm Summit would in turn lead in 1987 to the Brundtland Commission and its famous definition of sustainability, as noted above, is a society that "meets the needs of the present without compromising the ability of future generations to meet their own needs".

And it would lead to the Rio de Janeiro Earth Summit in 1992, which gave birth to UN conventions on climate change, biodiversity and desertification, and the Agenda 21 "roadmap" to sustainable development.

Both NEPA and the Stockholm conference were early steps in recognizing the integration of economic, environmental and social action, and the need for actions going beyond just regulating single pollutants.

The importance of taking steps to look at things in an integrated manner was something I learned while teaching in Georgia in the 1970s.

Tools for Decision-makers: Alan Hecht and Newt Gingrich in Carrollton Georgia

When the EPA was created, I started my teaching career as an Assistant Professor in the Department of Geology at West Georgia College (now the University of West Georgia) in Carrollton, Georgia. On the faculty of West Georgia College was Newt Gingrich who was a young assistant professor in the history department.

Newt did not have a long list of scholarly publications, so the department denied him tenure. He then moved to the geography department and pursued a career in politics, running to be a Congressman from the area. He made it on his third attempt.

While I was in Georgia, the Lower Chattahoochee Area Planning and Development Commission began studying land use issues. Newt Gingrich and I had the idea of conducting a land use study for Harris County that applied new methodologies of land use analysis.

Our proposed land study, funded by the Callaway Educational Foundation drew on the early work of Ian McHarg who was a land use planner and who developed a multidimensional system for land use management. His technique of "red-green" analysis aimed to help in making decisions by using what we now call a decision-support tool.[5]

For example, for a county manager charged with selecting a site for a new landfill, McHarg suggested the following technique. First, make a long list of every geological, environmental, social, and economic condition that might be important for picking a site. For example, a site whose groundwater table is far below the surface is good; a site where the groundwater is just below the surface is bad.

Then the county manager would create individual maps for each of the criteria and color good features green and bad features red. Laying the maps one on top of the other creates a multidimensional framework. The safest site will have the greenest areas; the riskiest sites have only red areas.

Today this can be easily handled by high tech computers, but in the 1970s I was thankful I had a class of students to do it.

In the conclusion of our 1973 Harris County report, I wrote:

> "The most urgent recommendation in this report is that public officials take specific actions to plan for the future. The warning signs are up. They indicate that a failure to engage in active planning for Harris Country will result in the gradual extension of urban sprawl first from Columbus and later from Atlanta. If this is permitted to happen, in a few years we will look back with nostalgia and sadness on the opportunity we missed for creating the highest quality of life for Harris County citizens."

The report had some remarkable insights. In simple terms it said, we need to think about the future, seek public input on future land use strategies, recognize resource limitations and best uses, establish a philosophical management approach (which today we might call "sustainable development") and develop a set of incentives, standards, and regulations to achieve these objectives.

More than 20 years later, I spoke at a conference in Atlanta, which at the time served to set many bad examples of urban sprawl. Had our recommendations been adopted Harris County would have been in better shape.

---

[5] Ian L. McHarg, *Design with Nature,* Garden City, N.Y., Doubleday/Natural History Press, 1969.

Historic Steps 1972 to 1992

One of the outcomes of the 1972 Stockholm Conference was to identify global population growth and urban development as a critical growing issue. Today the global population is expected to reach 9 billion by 2050 and 10 billion by 2100, with more people living in cities than ever before.

This prompted the retired UN Secretary General Ban Ki-moon (April 2015) to note that, "our struggle for global sustainability will be won or lost in cities."

Between the Stockholm Conference in 1972 and the Rio Summit in 1992, several major domestic and international events occurred, all shaping environmental protection and advancing the concept of sustainability.

On the domestic front, in 1972 Congress passed the Endangered Species Act and the Safe Drinking Water Act; on the international stage Switzerland organized Europe's first green party "The Popular Movement for the Environment."

More came from Congress in 1976 when they passed the "Resource Conservation and Recovery Act" (RCRA) giving EPA the authority to control hazardous waste from "cradle-to-grave." This includes the generation, transportation, treatment, storage, and disposal of hazardous waste. The RCRA also set forth a framework for the management of non-hazardous solid wastes.

Then in 1980 Congress passed "The Comprehensive Environmental Response, Compensation, and Liability Act" known as the Superfund Act, to help clean up uncontrolled or abandoned hazardous-waste sites as well as accidents, spills, and other emergency releases of pollutants and contaminants into the environment. EPA was given the power to seek out those parties responsible for any release and assure their cooperation in the cleanup.

The Report

Global

to the President

2000

ENTERING
THE
TWENTY-FIRST
CENTURY

Gerald O. Barney

See: https://www.elsevier.com/books/the-global-2000-report-to-the-president-of-the-us/barney/978-0-08-024618-5

Besides superfund sites, the 1980s were still a time of increasing environmental stresses for then and the future. Warning signals flashed in a 1980 CEQ report entitled *The Global 2000 Report to the President.* This Report was the first, and only, effort by the US to prepare a 20-year outlook on probable changes in the world's population, resources, economy, and environment.

The Report said: "If present trends continue, the world in 2000 will be more crowded, more polluted, less stable ecologically, and more vulnerable to disruption than the world we live in now." And, highlighting elements of the need for sustainable management, the CEQ Report said

> "The earth's carrying capacity—the ability of biological systems to provide resources for human need—is eroding" caused by a "progressive degradation and impoverishment of the earth's natural resource base."

Addressing international issues, the Report said efforts were far short of what was needed.

In 1981 another CEQ report, "Global Futures: Time to Act," emphasized the idea of sustainable development in an international context. The report said "The key concept here is sustainable development. Economic development, if it is to be successful over the long term, must proceed in a way that protects the natural resource base of developing countries."

And in 1987, UNEP had prepared their historic Report on sustainability and began planning for the 1992 Earth Summit in Rio.

For me, my teaching days in Georgia ended in 1976 when I came to the National Science Foundation (NSF) and ultimately to the EPA in 1989. At EPA, I was the Deputy Assistant Administrator in the Office of International Activities and had a lead role in planning for and participating in the 1992 Rio Earth Summit, as discussed in the next chapter.

CHAPTER TWO

THE 1987 UN REPORT "OUR COMMON FUTURE" AND THE 1992 RIO EARTH SUMMIT

During the 1980s and 1990s it was the international community that was advancing the goals of sustainability. In December 1983, the Secretary General of the United Nations, Javier Perez de Cuellar, asked the Prime Minister of Norway, Gro Harlem Brundtland to lead an independent group and develop a Report (*Our Common Future*) on environmental and developmental problems and solutions.

The UN mandated the Brundtland Commission to:

1. Reexamine the critical issues of environment and development and to formulate innovative, concrete, and realistic action proposals to deal with them;
2. Strengthen international cooperation on environment and development and to assess and propose new forms of cooperation that can break out of existing patterns and influence policies and events in the direction of needed change; and
3. Raise the level of understanding and commitment to action on the part of individuals, voluntary organizations, businesses, institutes, and governments.

This classic report was based on a UN resolution on the "Process of preparation of the Environmental Perspective to the Year 2000 and beyond."

Former EPA Administrator Bill Ruckelshaus was a member of the Brundtland Commission, supported by funding from a sustainability leader, Proctor and Gamble (P&G).

See: https://en.wikipedia.org/wiki/Our_Common_Future

The Report, proposing long-term environmental strategies for achieving sustainable development to the year 2000 and beyond, made a classic statement:

> **"Sustainable development is a process of change** in which the exploitation of resources, the direction of investments, the orientation of technological development; and institutional change are all in harmony and enhance both current and future potential to meet human needs and aspirations."

The concept of "process of change" is critical especially in anticipating future problems. The Report recognized that achieving this is not easy: "We do not pretend that the process is easy or straightforward; Painful choices have to be made. Thus, in the final analysis, sustainable development must rest on political will."

"Political will" is of course crucial. Chapter 4 showcases this for the EPA.

Recognizing a "sense of urgency," the Report noted that "the world must quickly design strategies that will allow nations to move from their present, often destructive, processes of growth and development onto sustainable development paths."

The UN Report is a classic work aiming to link environment and development as one single issue. This responded to its one critical mandate to "re-examine the critical issues of environment and development and to formulate innovative, concrete, and realistic action proposals to deal with them."

It is here that science and innovation are critical elements of promoting sustainability.

Following the publication of the 1987 UN report, the UN General Assembly voted to organize an Earth Summit in Rio de Janeiro on Environment and Development.

Gro Brundtland visiting with EPA Administrator Lisa Jackson in January 2012. Photograph by Alan Hecht.

Since preparing this Report, chairperson Gro Brundltand has continued to work to advance its many goals. In 2012 while she was in the US, I had the pleasure of arranging her visit to EPA and her meeting with EPA Administrator Lisa Jackson. She also spoke to the EPA on the critical need to enhance progress toward sustainability. Today Lisa Jackson is Apple's vice president of Environment, Policy and Social Initiatives.

The UN Report did focus a lot on developing countries as well as looking ahead to new challenges. The Report noted that the "world must quickly design strategies that will allow nations to move from their present, often destructive, processes of growth and development onto sustainable development paths. This will require policy changes in all countries, with respect both to their own development and to their impacts on other nations' development possibilities."

More on this would now be addressed by the Rio Summit in 1992.

The 1992 Rio Earth Summit

The United Nations Conference on Environment and Development (UNCED), also known as the Rio Earth Summit happened in October 1992. All the planning for Rio fell on Maurice Strong who deserves a great deal of credit for his international work.

For the Rio Summit, planning was intense aiming not only to finish negotiating a framework agreement on climate (discussed in Chapter 6) but also negotiate an agreement on protecting biological diversity and preparing a global development plan known as Agenda 21.

In planning for the Rio event, different regions had different priorities. African nations wanted poverty eradication. Asian nations wanted to control and protect their forests. Desertification was affecting dozens of countries and threatening arable land. At least all countries were concerned about air pollution and the control of toxic chemicals.

Major industrial countries and several developing countries were the dominant players in planning for the Rio meeting. The US was of course number one, and there was great pressure on President George H. Bush to attend.

While in 1989 President Bush was talking about being the environmental President, he had strong concerns about economic impacts of regulating Greenhouse Gases (GHG) and was not prepared to make formal commitments in a climate agreement. His participation in the Rio meeting was very much dependent on the outcome of ongoing climate negotiations, which is discussed in Chapter 6.

However, one area where President Bush did advance environmental goals was in protecting forests, and he used the Rio meeting to launch his "Forest for the Future" initiative.

Japan was also a key leader in Rio and came with a plan called "New Earth 21." Japan laid out plans for the world community to adopt goals for each of the next decades. They promoted using technology and innovation to advance business and environmental objectives. Writing in *The New Yorker* (June 1, 1992) John Newhouse said: "To the untutored eye, New Earth 21 is dazzling in its scope and its assumption about using new and improved technologies to lofty goals in fixed periods of time."

Over time, this of course would be a key objective for both business and government. In the world today, the concept and operation of "Smart Cities" are based on improved technology. The Smart Cities Council is today a global group to advance a city's "livability, workability and sustainability." For more on this go to: http://smartcitiescouncil.com/.

The European Commission (EC) was also a key leader in Rio pushing both a cap on carbon emissions and supporting additional resources to the developing world.

EPA Administrator William Reilly headed the US Delegation, which was a big coup for the EPA. Assistant Secretary of State Buff (Curtis) Bohlen was one of the alternate heads of the delegation along with several others including future US trade representative and World Bank President Robert Zoellick. Chief among the Congressional attendees were Senators Al Gore and the late Senator John Chafee.

Senator Chafee, Bill Reilly, and Al Gore (Photograph by EPA)

Life in Rio

Rio is predominantly a beach town, with a beach-like mentality. Even on cooler and rainy days, men in wet suits carry their surfboards through the business streets of the Leblon neighborhood.

I made many trips to Rio and it became one of my favorite cities.

Despite the appearance of a good and prosperous life on the beaches of Rio, key characteristics of life in the developing world abound. In the days leading up to the Earth Summit, one of the biggest problems in Rio was the great many children living on the streets or descending during the day from the *favelas* (slums), which covered the hills of the city. The kids infested the beaches and were a major cause of street crime. For the Rio Summit, the Brazilian government rounded up the street children and moved them out of the city, creating an artificial impression of a crime-free environment. When the conference ended, the kids returned.

Walking around Rio makes it clear that it is a city having trouble coping with environmental and social problems. In 1992 and today Rio is not alone as a city struggling with rapidly increasing population growth and social issues.

Twenty years later, in preparation for the Rio Earth Summit in 2012, the US and Brazil established a Joint Initiative on Urban Sustainability (JIUS) as a public-private partnership supporting investment in sustainable urban infrastructure. It was established by President Obama and Brazil's President

Dilma Rousseff in 2011 and officially launched by the former Administrator Lisa Jackson and the then Brazilian Minister of Environment Izabella Teixeira.

The JIUS brought together government, community and industry leaders from the United States and Brazil to generate economic growth, create decent jobs, eradicate poverty and protect the environment by increasing investment in green infrastructure and city-scale green technology strategies.

In Rio, there is a stark contrast between rich and poor. One of Rio's most affluent business-environmentalists, whom I often visited, operated from a well-furnished and secure house in a Rio suburb. All around the city are elegant homes and protected mansions. However, in the hills above Rio are millions of people living in favelas. I never ventured very far up into the favelas because embassy staff said they were unsafe.

Agenda 21

One major focus of the Rio Summit was to launch a new era of sustainable development. The Conference prepared a non-binding agreement called Agenda 21. The document's 40-plus chapters covered issues ranging from combating poverty, changing consumption patterns, monitoring population and demographic dynamics, promoting health and sustainable settlement patterns, and integrating environment and development into decision-making.

The preamble of Agenda 21 identified the same array of problems faced by society today:

> "Humanity stands at a defining moment in history. We are confronted with a perpetuation of disparities between and within nations, a worsening of poverty, hunger, ill health and illiteracy, and the continuing deterioration of the ecosystems on which we depend for our well-being. However, integration of environment and development concerns and greater attention to them can contribute to fulfilling basic needs, improving living standards, better managing and protecting ecosystems, and providing a safer, more prosperous future. No nation can achieve this on its own—but together we can—in a global partnership for sustainable development."

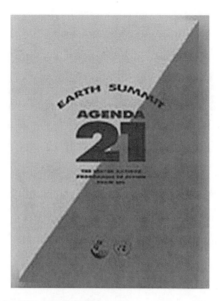

See: https://en.wikipedia.org/wiki/Agenda_21

Agenda 21 is a **non-binding international agreement** that offered recommendations that nations, states or local governments could adopt. As noted by Russell Train (in an article in the EPA journal in October 1992): "The coming together of more than 170 nations under the auspices of the Earth Summit was, if nothing else, the first global acknowledgment that environmental quality and economic well-being of the Earth's people depend directly on the continued health of its natural resources."

With US support, the conference also adopted a set of principles aiming to balance economic growth, development, environmental protection, and national and multilateral responsibilities. The goal was to get all advocates of the positions to agree on common goals.

The guts of Agenda 21 were good scientific, policy and management recommendations, not at odds with existing conservation and environmental laws. Among the principles of Agenda 21 were:

Principle 1: "Human beings are at the center of concerns for sustainable development." This principle makes clear that human well-being and quality of life are the objective of sustainability. This declaration reflects the principles of NEPA. Achieving sustainable development requires recognizing the need to balance the conservation of resources while protecting humans from the uncertainties of nature.

Principle 3: Intergenerational equity: "to equitably meet developmental and environmental needs of present and future generations" is again similar to NEPA and implicit in nearly all US laws related to the environment.

Principle 4: "To achieve sustainable development, environmental protection shall constitute an integral part of the development process and cannot be considered in isolation from it." Here we are talking about integrated decision-making, linking the social, environmental, and economic decision-making.

Principle 15: Precautionary approach. "Where there are threats of serious or irreversible damage, lack of full scientific certainty shall not be used as a reason for postponing cost-effective measures to prevent environmental degradation." The US Clean Air Act and other environmental laws enable the adoption of standards based on the possibility of harm rather than complete certainty.

After the Conference, the Commission on Sustainable Development (CSD) was created in December 1992 to ensure the effective follow-up of UNCED, to monitor and report on implementation of the agreements at the local, national, regional and international levels.

In the US, a post Rio Summit House Congressional Resolution (# 353, October 2012) expressed the view that "the United States should assume a strong leadership role in implementing the decisions made at the Earth Summit by developing a national strategy to implement Agenda 21 and other Earth summit agreements through domestic policy and foreign policy, by cooperating with all countries to identify and initiate further agreements to protect the global environment, and by supporting and participating in a high-level United Nations Sustainable Development Commission."

Congress urged support for financing initiatives, climate change mitigation, prevention of biodiversity loss, a strong international legal framework, promotion of public participation in environmental decision-making, prevention of deforestation and marine pollution, energy conservation, and a series of goals relating to sustainable development.

Political Craziness

As an example of the craziness of politics, and stress on the career work force, Agenda 21 has been treated by many conservatives as an **economic and political threat to society.**

One famous attack was from Glenn Beck who put Agenda 21 on the cover of his magazine *The Blaze*, in a 2012 issue and had an article exposing what he thought of as a "global scheme that has the potential to wipe out freedoms of all US citizens."

Beck followed up with a book attacking Agenda 21.

In the 2012 Presidential election campaign, the Republican National Committee also adopted a resolution against Agenda 21 saying, "Sustainable development is a threat to the American way of life."

This crazy resolution said:

WHEREAS, the United Nations Agenda 21 is a comprehensive plan of **extreme environmentalism, social engineering, and global political control.**

WHEREAS, this United Nations Agenda 21 plan **of radical so-called "sustainable development" views the American way of life of private property ownership, single family homes, private car ownership and individual travel choices, and privately-owned farms; all as destructive to the environment.**

RESOLVED, the Republican National Committee recognizes the **destructive and insidious nature** of United Nations Agenda 21 and hereby exposes to the public and public policy makers the dangerous intent of the plan.

RESOLVED, that the federal and state and local governments across the country **be well informed of the underlying harmful implications of implementation of United Nations Agenda 21 destructive strategies for "sustainable development"** and we hereby endorse rejection of its radical policies and rejection of any grant monies attached to it.

See: http://www.rosakoire-bgm.com/

Big Success of Rio: Business Leadership on Sustainability

Opposite the political craziness cited above, Agenda 21 and the Rio Summit did motivate very important actions on sustainability, one of the most important outcomes being the creation of the World Business Council for Sustainable Development (WBCSD).

The author and founder of the BCSD Stephen Schmidheiny argued that for companies to successfully compete domestically and internationally they must adapt to new market conditions, which include concerns about the environmental impacts of their products as well as their process and production methods.

In organizing the BCSD, he recognized the commercial and environmental benefits of the "greening of industry" and became a strong advocate for sustainable development and industrial ecology. This continued to build on work that had already begun in the European Union.

See: https://mitpress.mit.edu/books/changing-course

Schmidheiny and the Business Council in turn prepared a book called *Changing Course* that outlined a business perspective for sustainable development. This remarkable book said, "Business will play a vital role in the future health of this planet," saying that the business world was committed to sustainable development.

The Council correctly noted that "new forms of cooperation between government, business and society are needed to achieve this goal."

A cover story on the Rio Summit ("Growth vs. Development") Business Week on May 11, said that world leaders would **seek a route to prosperity without environmental degradation.** This is in fact a crucial point that sustainable development is not a threat to the economy. Yet the article was clever enough to note that the concept of sustainable development could generate plenty of controversy. This is true today.

Then and today, the WBCSD is a leader aiming to:

- Be a leading business advocate on sustainable development;
- Participate in policy development to create the framework conditions for business to make an effective contribution to sustainable human progress;
- Develop and promote the business case for sustainable development;
- Demonstrate the business contribution to sustainable development solutions and share leading edge practices among members;
- Contribute to a sustainable future for developing nations and nations in transition.

In 2000, the European Union (EU) began promoting sustainability as something positive for business. An EU Strategy adopted in Lisbon in 2000 set the goal for the EU to become the most competitive and dynamic knowledge-based economy in the world. The European Council has stated, "Clear and stable objectives for sustainable development would present significant economic opportunities and the potential to unleash a new wave of technology innovation, generating growth and employment."

From 2000 on, business support for sustainable development has grown steadily. Many businesses recognized the importance of sustainable practices to support a growing economy. Reducing the use of resources typically leads to reduced purchasing and operating costs, so companies generally view sustainable development as enhancing their bottom line while reducing their environmental footprint.

In addition, sustainability enhances shareholder value by improving brand image, reputation, and stakeholder relationships. According to the Dow Jones Sustainability Indexes: "Sustainability is a business approach that creates long-term shareholder value by embracing opportunities and managing risks that derive from economic, environmental and social developments."

Today this view of sustainability as an economic strategy is becoming more widespread in industry. After examining sustainability initiatives in energy and manufacturing at 30 large corporations, a 2009 study published in the *Harvard Business Review* concluded that

"Sustainability is a mother lode of organizational and technological innovations that yield both bottom-line and top-line returns" and that "there is no alternative to sustainable development."[6]

The business world links sustainability and income which are mutually supportive. Hence, sustainable development is generally viewed as enhancing the bottom line while reducing their global footprint.

Post Rio Federal Action: EPA Report to Congress

Following the Rio Summit, EPA Administrator Bill Reilly gave a summary of his observations to the House Committee on Foreign Relations. He argued that the conference was a big success. In a summary for the then-existing *EPA Journal* (September-October 1992) he wrote "The Earth Summit presented unprecedented opportunities for governments of all nations, at all levels, to pursue strategies for sustainable development. The question we must ask ourselves today is: How do we expand our economies to meet the aspirations of our people, while still protecting human health and the natural resources on which lasting economic growth depends? How well we answer this question will define our quality of life in the 21st century."

Reilly did note that countries agreed on follow-up activities and established the UN Commission on Sustainable Development (CSD) which for the next 20 years would advance and monitor progress on implementing the goals of Agenda 21.

Following the 1992 Rio Summit, Congress asked EPA to explain its role in sustainable development. Congress was "interested in EPA's effort to explore the concept of sustainable development." The Committee was particularly interested in how environmental concerns can be best incorporated in national, state and local development and economic planning and decision-making processes.

This was the first time that EPA addressed how to incorporate sustainability into its overall management.

In replying to Congress, EPA prepared a report "**Sustainable Development and the Environmental Protection Agency**" that acknowledged the importance of achieving sustainability but noting that EPA "has not

---

[6] Ram Nidumolu, E., K. Prahald, and M. R. Rangaswami, 2009, "Sustainability is now the key driver of innovation." *Harvard Business Journal*, September.

employed the concept of sustainability explicitly in an overall policy framework or programmatic objective."

Instead, EPA has "developed its programs and projects primarily to fulfill statutory mandates that do not specify sustainability as an objective."

EPA acknowledges that it "has not employed the concept of sustainability explicitly in an overall policy framework or programmatic objective." EPA said this reflected the "minor role that sustainability plays in EPA's statutory authority" and that "the full scope of planning and implementation of sustainable development policies extended well beyond the purview of EPA."

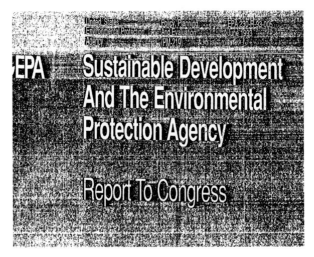

In looking ahead, it also noted that "sustainability programs should not duplicate existing programs such as the recently created Pollution Prevention Program."

This comment was rather short sighted, when you realize the goal of reducing and/or recycling waste and pollution is a first step toward achieving sustainable practices. Why aim merely to reduce toxic waste when we can eliminate it with new chemicals and processes?

The 1993 Report did conclude that the concept of sustainable development "provides a useful framework for discussion of the Nation's long-term environment and economic priorities" but also noted that "these concepts have not been developed yet to the extent that they provide a basis for

EPA operational planning."

EPA noted that while "the precise meaning of sustainable development is still the subject of scientific and political discussion, consensus does exist on several of its fundamental principles. First, sustainable development requires a long-term perspective for planning and policy development; Second, sustainable development must build on and reinforce the interdependence of our economy and our environment; Third, sustainable development calls for new, integrative approaches to achieve economic, social and environmental objectives."

The EPA report also noted that enhancing public awareness and participation was critical, noting "that the nation can only achieve and maintain sustainable development when its citizens understand this concept and embrace it as a national priority."

Looking ahead, EPA advised Congress that it would seek a dialogue with the public, Congress, and other government agencies to identify ways to integrate sustainable development into both the Agency's operations and national environmental and economic policy.

The final Report also noted that broad objectives, like sustainable development, require anticipatory and integrated approaches to environmental problems.

In hindsight, the EPA report failed to recognize the important role that EPA science and technology could play in achieving sustainability. Movement in this direction would make a big difference in shaping future EPA activities.

President's Commission on Sustainable Development (PCSD)

During the next Administration President Clinton in 1993 established the Council on Sustainable Development (PCSD) to advise him on "bold, new approaches to achieve our economic, environmental, and equity goals."

The PCSD lasted for more than five years aiming to advance the goals of Agenda 21. Their mission was defined to:

- Forge consensus on Policy by bringing together diverse interests to identify and develop innovative economic, environmental and social policies and strategies;
- Demonstrate the Implementation of policy that fosters sustainable development by working with diverse interests to identify and demonstrate the implementation of sustainable development;
- Get the word out about sustainable development; and
- Valuate and report on progress by recommending national, community, and enterprise level frameworks for tracking sustainable development.

One PCSD goal was to "Encourage people to work together to create healthy communities where natural and historic resources are preserved, jobs are available, sprawl is contained, neighborhoods are secure, education is lifelong, transportation and health care are accessible, and all citizens have opportunities to improve the quality of their lives."

It was nice having an Administration that recognized the value of sustainable development and the need to link business and government practices.

This does not seem to be the case for the Trump Administration. Green Biz Chairman Joel Makower said in a 2017 tweet: "Let's face it folks, Donald Trump is sustainability's stress test."

Maybe so, but the reality of life today requires more than ever before a resilient and sustainable society. This will be clear in the last chapter of this book.

Post Clinton Administration there was still much to overcome in advancing the goals of sustainability, especially at the EPA. More on this is in Chapter 4.

For now, let's turn to the next big international event in 2002.

CHAPTER THREE

THE 2002 JOHANNESBURG WORLD SUMMIT ON SUSTAINABLE DEVELOPMENT (WSSD)

International attention on sustainability continued and ten years later, the next international conference, called the World Summit on Sustainable Development (WSSD) convened in Johannesburg, South Africa.

In October 2001, I left EPA to go on a two-year detail to the White House with a dual role of serving as environmental advisor on the National Security Council (NSC) and as Assistant Director for Sustainable Development at the Council on Environmental Quality (CEQ). During my White House tenure, I managed a suite of environmental issues and acted as White House coordinator of preparations for the Johannesburg Summit.

Sadly, on 9/11/2001 the FBI was interviewing me for the White House assignment when the first aircraft crashed into the World Trade Center. For a few minutes, we watched the TV, then grimly the agent looked at me and said "this interview is over."

In the period between 2000 and 2002, several international meetings occurred to advance elements of sustainability. One important meeting was the **UN Millennium Summit in 2000**. Here 189 countries, including the US, adopted the eight UN Millennium Development Goals (MDG).

The 8 goals had 21 targets and 60 indicators of success by 2015.

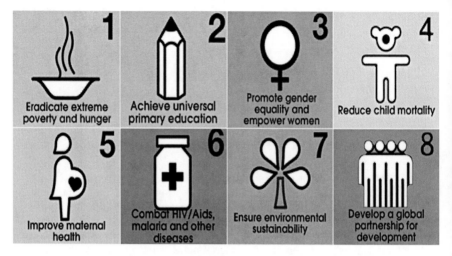

See: https://en.wikipedia.org/wiki/Millennium_Development_Goals.

One of the important conclusions of the MDG was the need for shared responsibilities among nations and the need for global partnerships, a theme that would dominate the WSSD.

By 2014, there was significant progress in achieving each of these goals, and by 2015 the UN moved on and adopted Sustainable Development Goals, discussed in Chapter 7.

The **WSSD** meeting in Johannesburg, building on the Millennium Goals focused on the linkages of economic, social and environmental development and by advancing a new concept of global partnerships.

White House Planning for the WSSD

October 1, 2001 was my first day in the White House and the next day was my first staff meeting at the CEQ. Planning for the WSSD was just getting started and Jim Connaughton, the chairman of the CEQ and Paula Dobriansky, the Undersecretary of State for Global Affairs, co-chaired a White House planning group. Connaughton formally announced that I would be the executive secretary to the planning group.

While my role was *coordinator* I tried in every way, drawing on my experience as head of the NCPO, to influence policy. From day one at the White House, I had some sense of the underlying intrigue and politics lurking in the shadows. My early interaction at the NSC made it clear that planning for WSSD and advancing sustainability would not be easy. One day an NSC colleague came into my office and anxiously asked, "What the hell did we commit to in Rio?"

It was clear to me that the US needed a WSSD game plan. Hence, I proposed to draft such a plan and much to my surprise was given the assignment.

In my plan, I proposed three objectives that might appeal to the White House: (1) advance global partnerships, (2) emphasize the important of alleviating poverty and social unrest, and (3) creating a global environment of hope and optimism about the future.

While the WSSD was an international meeting, I argued that the US domestic audience would use the event to judge the commitment of this Administration to sustainable development and environmental stewardship.

At the time I was writing my memo, government agencies looked to the White House for a clear sense of the WSSD goals, and what their roles would be. Outside of government, stakeholders each had a different view of the WSSD and this led me to wrestle with balancing a mixture of perspectives.

One key issue among all stakeholders was financial and technical assistance from the rich to the poor. Many Liberals on the Hill were arguing that while in the past decade there had been strong economic growth, the environment has suffered and the world's poor have gotten poorer. They wanted new increased foreign aid and new US leadership to solve global problems and support new environmental initiatives that spur new technologies and create new export opportunities.

Non-governmental organizations (NGO), who were painting a grim picture of the world, also wanted increased foreign aid to help reduce the number of people living in poverty around the world.

From outside the US, the European Union saw the upcoming WSSD as another opportunity to demonstrate global leadership and criticize the US for its lack of commitment to climate change and its resistance to increased foreign aid. The EU wanted a global focus on sustainable development. They were willing to double the amount of foreign aid.

None of the above was supported by Conservatives who opposed any new binding agreements.

US Vision for the WSSD

I proposed a US vision statement for WSSD and in my first draft, I wrote, "Sustainable development begins at home. All countries must take ownership of sustainable development by building enduring institutions and by adopting, the right domestic economic, environmental and social policies. There can be no sustainable development without a national commitment to good governance, and enforcement of sound economic, social and environmental policies."

My memo laid out several actions, called "tasks," aimed at outreach to nongovernment and business leaders and convergence on key policy objectives. Among my proposed tasks were actions sensitive to the fact that the meeting would be held in Africa where many countries were experiencing problems facing developing countries.

- The White House/President meets with key business and finance leaders to promote sustainable development themes, including environmental management systems, responsible corporate management, and environmental stewardship.
- The White House/President meets with faith based and charity organizations and foundations to support their efforts at promoting poverty alleviation, sustainable development, education and children's health.
- The White House/President meets with key African American CEOs, business and religious leaders, and foundations to signal US interest in WSSD and Africa.
- The CEQ Chairman signals US strong support for WSSD, giving speeches that WSSD is important, the US is concerned about developing country issues, the US is working with allies to make the WSSD a success, and the US is beginning to consult with NGOs and the private sector.
- The State Department meets with allies to develop a focused WSSD message on economic growth, poverty alleviation and sustainable development.
- The State and the Agency for International Development (AID) develop a paper on US assistance to Africa drawing on the African

Growth and Development Act, Trade Agreements, technical assistance, capacity building, and AID's support.

- The State, AID and EPA prepare compelling case studies that show how good governance and rule of law lead to sustainable development.
- The AID, Treasury, and State prepare a paper on what the US is doing for poverty alleviation through debt relief, capacity building, technical assistance, and financial support.
- The AID should prepare a paper on how US technical assistance and financial aid are helping to fight poverty and build good governance in developing countries.
- The State, EPA and AID, and HHS prepare a paper on what the US is doing to advance education and protect children's health.
- The CEQ develops a legislative package to ratify pending treaties and legislative changes to implement agreements for announcement at the WSSD.

As you can imagine, my proposed tasks got a lot of attention. In February 2002, the NSC scheduled a WSSD meeting with political leaders. I was not included but my boss, CEQ Director Jim Connaughton said there were big "Ps" (i.e. political people) and little "Ps" and that I was a little "p."

I was not upset at being a little "p". I did not support much of the environmental policy in the Bush Administration. As a career person, I offered the White House staff my best guidance, and hoped to have some positive impact on decision-making.

Being a little "p" was just fine with me.

By early February, it was clear that President Bush would not go to the WSSD. Vice President Cheney was a possibility, but there seemed to be some thinking about appointing a special WSSD envoy. Secretary of State Powell was ready to go and ultimately, he would lead the US delegation.

At this time, I sat down with senior State Department and White House staff to draft a US vision statement for WSSD. I started the first draft with the phrase "Sustainability begins at home." I included a paragraph on actions taken by US state and domestic agencies in supporting sustainability. Then I moved on to the international issues. The drafting team would work on this for the next weeks.

All subsequent drafts retained my first sentence but eliminated references to domestic actions. I saw this as a serious mistake. However, nothing I could do would change this.

As we were preparing our goals for the WSSD, the EU was bashing the US at almost every meeting for the US lack of commitment to sustainability. I argued to Connaughton that the US was doing a great deal, although largely at the state level. I argued we could do a great deal more by pushing federal sustainability policies.

Unfortunately, this view had no attraction in the White House that equated "sustainability" with regulating climate emissions. While the phrase "sustainability begins at home" survived, it meant, "You in the developing world need to get your act together." Frustrated by all of this I would ultimately return to EPA with the goal of leading an effort on sustainability.

While the White House was working on defining the US position for WSSD and drafting a vision statement, the State Department staff were attending all the international negotiating sessions and trying to move toward closure, on what would be called the Implementation Plan. By April, one concept seemed to have growing support among all participants and this was around the idea of global voluntary "partnerships." The State was reporting to me that the US could really lead on this if it got out front.

By April, the vision statement was finally coming together and by May, the President had asked Secretary Powell to lead the delegation. Now the Vision Statement was public:

> *"We believe* **sustainable development begins at home and is supported by effective domestic policies, and international partnerships.** Self-governing people prepared to participate in an open world marketplace are the very foundation of sustainable development. President Bush has emphasized that the hopes of all people, no matter where they live, lie in greater political and economic freedom, the rule of law, and good governance."

The fourth and final preparatory conference for WSSD convened in Bali, Indonesia from May 27 to June 7, 2002. The Bali meeting came close to approving a final WSSD Agreement. The good news was an overall agreement to advance the concept of "partnerships" which was emerging as a new type of UN activity. Between the Bali meeting and the WSSD, Washington worked hard pulling together partnerships on water, health and other areas, which could make the WSSD meeting a big success.

Johannesburg (Joburg)

The meeting occurred at a time of severe drought in Africa, and many side meetings talked about emergency food aid. The US was eager to help Africa with food imports but ran into a serious problem with concerns about the "genetically" modified food sources.

UN Secretary General Kofi Annan wrote to President Bush on July 30 requesting the President's help in addressing the food crises in South Africa. The President responded on August 31 saying that the US had begun to provide food as early as February. However, "unfortunately misleading and scientifically unfounded statements about the safety of the US bio-engineered corn, including statements by UN officials caused some governments in the region to refuse the food." (Quote from an unclassified cable in my files.)

The President went on to say that "it is very disturbing that this food, which has been consumed daily by millions of Americans for years with no adverse consequences, is being withdrawn from vulnerable people." The President asked Kofi Annan to help allay concerns about the safety of US food and address the humanitarian crises.

Once the Conference began, at a major plenary session, Secretary of State Powell spoke saying, "The US is taking actions to meet environmental challenges, including climate change." Unfortunately, booing and hecklers interrupted his speech several times yelling "Shame on Bush." South African Foreign Minister Nkosazana Dlamini-Zuma who was chairing the session called on hecklers to stop and called their outbursts "totally unacceptable." After Powell finished, a frustrated and somber US delegation rushed to leave.

During much of the meeting Paula Dobriansky of the State Department and Jim Connaughton of the CEQ as well as EPA Administrator Christie Todd Whitman and Secretary of State Colin Powell attended many side events.

Paula Dobriansky of State and Jim Connaughton from CEQ—Photograph by Alan Hecht.

EPA Administrator Christie Todd Whitman and Secretary Powell at WSSD Seminar sponsored by the Smithsonian (photograph by Alan Hecht)

In the end, the WSSD negotiated and adopted two documents: a "Plan of Implementation" and the "Johannesburg Declaration on Sustainable Development." The Plan of Implementation was designed as a framework for action to implement the commitments originally agreed at UNCED. The Johannesburg Declaration outlined the path taken from UNCED to the WSSD, highlighted present challenges, expressed a commitment to sustainable development, underscored the importance of multilateralism and emphasized the need for implementation.

The Declaration highlighted the previous conferences in Stockholm and Rio, including the following:

- Thirty years ago, in Stockholm, we agreed on the urgent need to respond to the problem of environmental deterioration. Ten years ago, at the United Nations Conference on Environment and Development, held in Rio de Janeiro, we agreed that the protection of the environment and social and economic development are fundamental to sustainable development, based on the Rio Principles. To achieve such development, we adopted the global program entitled Agenda 21 and the Rio Declaration on Environment and Development, 3 to which we reaffirm our commitment. The Rio Conference was a significant milestone that set a new agenda for sustainable development.
- At the Johannesburg Summit, we have achieved much in bringing together a rich tapestry of peoples and views in a constructive search for a common path towards a world that respects and implements the vision of sustainable development. The Johannesburg Summit has also confirmed that significant progress has been made towards achieving a global consensus and partnership among all the people of our planet.

The WSSD did end with a strong focus on partnerships and sustainability

- We welcome the focus of the Johannesburg Summit on the indivisibility of human dignity and are resolved, through decisions on targets, timetables and partnerships, to speedily increase access to such basic requirements as clean water, sanitation, adequate shelter, energy, health care, food security and the protection of biodiversity. At the same time, we will work together to help one another gain access to financial resources, benefit from the opening of markets, ensure capacity-building, use modern technology to bring about development and make sure that there is technology transfer, human resource development, education and training to banish underdevelopment forever.

On WSSD, the US said it would "work to unite governments, the private sector and civil society to strengthen domestic institutions of governance, open markets and mobilize and use all development resources more effectively."

The WSSD was largely concerned with implementation rather than with new visions, treaties and agreements. It did lead to four US commitments made by Secretary Powell in his opening remarks: "We have unveiled at this conference four new 'signature' partnerships in water, energy, agriculture, and forests. These programs will expand access to clean water and affordable energy, reduce pollution, provide jobs, and improve food supplies for millions."

The **Water for the Poor** Initiative aimed to address the fact that more than 1 billion people lacked access to clean water. While this was the largest US initiative, it was primarily a composite of existing AID activities that were highly decentralized and poorly coordinated. In effect, the AID simply renamed its sprawling water programs the Water for the Poor Initiative. However, the new partnership between the Centers for Disease Control and AID promoted safe water through low-tech, locally produced decontamination agents and water storage improvements. The Water for the Poor Initiative also stimulated other business and foundation efforts to provide portable water in Africa, India and elsewhere.

The **Congo Basin Partnership** accomplished much partly due to support by the then Secretary of State Colin Powell and an existing intergovernmental program among African countries and non-governmental organizations. Among the results of this effort are additional protected areas in the Republic of the Congo, 10,000 square miles of national park areas in Gabon and the sustainable development of logging practices by companies in Central Africa. The United States committed to invest up to $53 million over the next four years to support sustainable forest management and a network of national parks and protected areas.

The **Clean Energy Initiative** bundled a diverse set of new and existing efforts under one umbrella. These included a Partnership for Clean Fuels, the Global Village Partnership (GVP) and the Efficient Energy for Sustainable Development Initiative. EPA played a key role in the first initiative aimed at eliminating leaded gasoline and reducing sulfur in diesel and gasoline fuels. Much to the success of this and other efforts as of January 1, 2006, all sub-Saharan Africa has stopped refining and importing leaded gasoline. The GVP has hosted dozens of workshops and focused on addressing energy needs for billions of people.

The **Initiative to Cut Hunger** in Africa aimed to advance technology sharing with small-scale farmers, strengthen agricultural policy development, fund higher education and regional technology collaboration; and expand resources for local infrastructure. For this project, the United States planned to invest some $90 million in 2003, including $53 million to bring science and technology for African farmers and $37 million to unleash the power of markets for small-scale agriculture.

Side Trip in Johannesburg

At the end of the WSSD Jim Connaughton and I visited Soweto (acronym for *southwest township),* the site of a slum community, where people live in one room shacks with no running water or sanitation. Water is available from city pumps scattered throughout the township. Water in South Africa is of high quality and purity and can be drunk from the tap, even in Soweto, although the bucket may not be clean. Hundreds of porta-johns scattered throughout the community provide sanitation. The government empties these facilities once a week. Visiting

Soweto strongly underscored the pain, suffering and need of development communities.

One year after WSSD, my tenure at CEQ ended and in June 2003 I returned to EPA and vowed to work on advancing the concept and practices of sustainable development. Since the Rio Summit in 1992 and following the WSSD Summit, States and cities were activity engaged in sustainability and it was at this point that I decided that EPA had to be a leader on sustainability.

The challenge ahead was how to make this happen.

Connaughton and Hecht in Soweta

CHAPTER FOUR

HISTORIC STEPS TO MAKING SUSTAINABILITY OPERATIONAL AT THE EPA

History is Important!

Now comes an important part of the history of how the EPA has adopted and implemented actions on sustainability. I want the public to fully appreciate what EPA is doing today—and what are the future challenges.

This is especially important now under the Trump Administration when EPA is under severe financial and staff reductions.

EPA's core mission is to protect human health and the environment. While the Agency is still under political attack for negative impacts on the economy—which is not true—it has evolved from a policeman in the 1970s to being a real science leader in promoting integrated resource management and protecting human health. Today EPA is very much concerned with dealing with problems of the 21st century that go beyond simply controlling pollutants. It wants very much to build a society that is sustainable, green and safe for human health.

Sustainability activities at EPA were advanced in part by the 1992 Rio Earth Summit and the post 2002 WSSD event, especially when many states and cities and businesses began making commitments to achieve sustainability development. In fact, today, many states and cities are clear leaders on advancing sustainability.

Then and now, Washington and Oregon have been leaders in the Pacific Northwest and the cities of Portland, Seattle, and Olympia, Washington had developed extensive forward-looking sustainability programs. There, and in many other states, architects, engineers, city planners, citizen groups, universities, and tribal communities are all working together in resource management and building design to improve quality of life and lessen environmental burdens.

In the Midwest, post WSSD, Minnesota had set 19 goals for the state's future and used 70 indicators to track progress. Among the set goals is that Minnesotans "will conserve natural resources to give future generations a healthy environment and a strong economy." Minneapolis and other Midwest cities were all competing for the unofficial title of most sustainable city.

In Chicago, the late Mayor Richard M. Daley (1902-1976), formed a sustainability team that worked hard to advance sustainability through procurement and engineering policies. In the East, New Jersey had been one of the nation's leading proponents for state-level green planning. New Jersey has also been an effective leader in adopting best practices from other US states and international cities.

And in Texas, the city of Austin had adopted the concept of sustainability as a guiding principle for development decisions.

Today, can you identify the top 15 sustainable cities in the US? Here is a summary from the web link: http://grist.org/article/2009-07-16-sustainable-green-us-cities/full/.

Seattle, San Francisco, Portland, Oakland, California, San Jose, California, Austin, Sacramento, Boston, Denver, Chicago, San Diego, New York, Los Angeles, Dallas, and Columbus Ohio.

In 2003, looking at what was going on in states and cities and in the business world, it was clear to me that the federal government needed to move in this direction. While I was on detail in the White House, I tried to advance the goal of sustainability based on what the states were doing.

I was not successful, and then made it my goal when I returned to EPA in 2003.

Making Sustainability an EPA Goal

In 2003, on the path back to EPA after my tenure in the White House, I met with Deputy Administrator Linda Fisher (who lately became the sustainability officer at DuPont) and proposed that the Agency take a lead on sustainability.

She agreed and said, much to my surprise and pleasure, that the head of the EPA Office of Research and Development (ORD) Paul Gilman (also shared the same view, arguing that working on the science of sustainability is a needed path forward.

Consequently, I moved back to EPA and became the first and only Director for Sustainable Development in the Office of Research and Development (ORD). Paul Gilman, who is now the Senior Sustainability Officer at Covanta, and I had the goal of making EPA the sustainability leader in the government. We saw science and technology as the key elements of planning a sustainable future.

For EPA, the challenge to bring all programs together and move toward sustainability was a challenge of addressing the many issues raised in EPA's Report to Congress in 1993.

- How can a regulatory agency whose historic roots lie in controlling pollution implement the concept of sustainability?
- How does an agency organized by individual media offices develop an integrated-systems approach to environmental protection?
- How does a federal agency without a specific mandate for sustainability promote and achieve sustainable development?

I knew this was not going to be easy, even though almost every Administration had inched forward on the idea. Clearly, we needed Administrative support, cross-program cooperation, and clear demonstrations of successes by cities and states in achieving sustainable outcomes.

Under the Bush Administration, Paul Gilman had a political advisor and communications director, Michael Brown, who confirmed to me in 2003 that the concept of sustainability had **"no political traction."**

By 2007, the atmosphere had slowly changed and Michael told me that it was **"OK to talk about sustainability."**

Beginning in 2003, we moved to make sustainability a key ORD and EPA goal.

Historic EPA Steps toward Sustainability

Over its long history, EPA has evolved from its original role as a policeman addressing single media issues to cross-media programs (linking air, water and land protection) enhancing strong stakeholder engagement in addressing environmental health and social issues and expanding science and technology.

Science is a key element of EPA's actions to advance understanding of complex relationships between human activities and impacts to health and the environment, and to promote innovative and sustainable solutions to 21st century environmental challenges.

Today, EPA is a critical agency in dealing with serious environment and health problems and is in no way a threat to the environment. Actions of the Agency are aimed to protect the environment in an integrated manner that links natural resources, human health, and economic growth. EPA recognizes that all parts of society—communities, individuals, businesses, and state, local and tribal governments—must work together, with good scientific information to make communities safe, sustainable and economically productive.

One impetus in advancing scientific tools for decision-making relates to a 1988 report from the House Committee on Science "Unlocking Our Future." Chairman of the Report, Congressman Sensenbrenner sent the Report to the Speaker Newt Gingrich, highlighting a "new science enterprise."

> "While acknowledging the continuing need for science and engineering in national security, health and the economy, the challenges we face today cause us to propose that the scientific and engineering enterprise ought to

move toward center stage in a fourth role; **that of helping society make good decisions. We believe this role for science will take on increasing importance, as we face difficult decisions related to the environment.**"

It is here that the concept and actions on building "decision support tools" were emphasized.

Actions we began in 2003 were built on steps taken by a past EPA administrator on expanding its role to risk assessor, promoting integrated management, linking environment and the economy, environmental stewardship, systems science and ultimately sustainability.

Integrated Management: Even President Nixon recognized the interconnectedness of the environment and the inherent cross-media nature of environmental protection. His plan to establish EPA noted that, for pollution control purposes, "the environment must be perceived as a single, interrelated system."

On the Agency's 15th anniversary, Russell E. Train who was the second Administrator of EPA (1973 to 1977) and who represented the US at the Stockholm Conference in 1972, reiterated the need for EPA to deal with the environment as an integrated system. He expressed concern with EPA's "compartmentalized nature" and its resulting ineffectiveness in dealing with pollutants, which "tend to move readily among air, water, and land."

Similarly, Administrator Lee Thomas (1985-1989) stressed the need for cross-media reviews so that "we don't just transfer pollutants from one medium to another."

From the above, it was clear to me and many others that **system thinking** and **integrated actions** on, air, water and land were critically needed. It was also clear to me that a key element of sustainability was to maximize the positive economic, social and environmental impacts of policy decisions.

Link of Environment and Economic Growth: In the early 1990s, Administrator Bill Reilly (1989-1993) highlighted the integral relationship between a healthy environment and a prosperous economy. He argued that economic activity depends on healthy natural systems and that economic growth can foster environmental protection. Reilly recognized the need "to develop systems of economic growth and activity that ensure sustainability."

Bill Reilly also articulated the need for a broad sustainability focus. He said, "I don't think we will be able to say, in the popular phrase of the moment that we have attained a sustainable level of development until we function in harmony with these ecosystems and learn to keep them productive. [EPA] is not, nor ought to be, fundamentally about reducing this effluent or that emission, but rather about protecting the totality of the environment."

Reilly was prophetic noting that:

> "When we look to the future, it's going to mean asking different kinds of questions: How will a product be used? How will it be manufactured? What kinds of wastes are created in its manufacture? And how will it be disposed of? Is it possible to create an alternative product, which entails significantly fewer environmental problems—a product which can be recycled, which is biodegradable, which minimizes or prevents altogether the resulting assaults on the environment?"

In the mid-1990s Administrator Carol Browner (1993-2001) further advanced the link between environmental protection and economic vibrancy. She advocated that sustainable development does not require "having to choose between a healthy environment and a healthy economy. It means having both."

Environmental Stewardship: In the 2000-decade, Administrator Mike Leavitt (2003-2005) advanced the concepts of collaborative problem solving and environmental stewardship. The concept of "collaborative conservation" was outlined in Executive Order 13352 (August 26, 2004) requiring EPA and four other agencies to "actively engage all stakeholders" when implementing conservation and environmental projects.[7]

This order was followed in 2005 by EPA Administrator Steve Johnson (2005-2009) who challenged the career staff of the Innovation Action Council (IAC) to develop an environmental stewardship strategy. In preparing this report, the IAC sought input both from within EPA and from state environmental commissioners, tribes, environmental experts, and opinion leaders.

In 2005 the IAC final report, *Everyday Choices: Opportunities for Environmental Stewardship*, linked the ideas of stewardship and sustainability, noting the need for new policy and technological innovation

---

[7] https://www.fedcenter.gov/Bookmarks/index.cfm?id=57.

and greater scientific understanding of the complex biosphere as well as support for responsible stewardship and decision-making by firms, investors, communities, and governments at all levels. This Report was the first explicit statement of EPA senior leadership focusing on recommendations for sustainability outcomes that the nation should seek.

This is turn must be supported by a stronger lead role for EPA on sustainability research. In telegraphing the evolution of EPA, Administrator Johnson (photo) said the Report is **"what I believe is the next step in an ongoing evolution of policy goals from pollution control to pollution prevention and sustainability."**

Sustainability Research: In much of its history, EPA recognized the need for science to move beyond the regulatory framework, and to develop and implement a more integrated, systems-based, and cross-media approach to better address the challenges of the new century.

This required that the agency's efforts be expanded to (1) collect, develop, synthesize, and disseminate integrated scientific and technical information; (2) develop metrics for determining progress toward national sustainability goals; and (3) develop cost-effective and innovative solutions consistent with smart economic growth.

During this period, the new discipline of *sustainability science* was emerging as a basis for sustainable solutions. Famed scientist Robert Kates (Kates et al. 2001) and a long list of distinguished colleagues identified seven critical questions concerning sustainability.[8] They were:

1. How can the dynamic interactions between nature and society—including lags and inertia—be better incorporated into emerging models and conceptualizations that integrate the Earth's system, human development, and sustainability?
2. How are long-term trends in environment and development, including consumption and population, reshaping nature-society interactions in ways relevant to sustainability?
3. What determines the vulnerability or resilience of the nature-society system, and in particular, what kinds of places and for particular types of ecosystems and human livelihoods?
4. Can scientifically meaningful "limits" or "boundaries" be defined that would provide an effective warning of conditions beyond which the nature-society systems incur a significantly increased risk of serious degradation?
5. What systems of incentive structures—including markets, rules, norms, and scientific information—can most effectively improve social capacity to guide interactions between nature and society toward more sustainable trajectories?
6. How can today's operational systems for monitoring and reporting on environmental and social conditions be integrated or extended to provide more useful guidance for efforts to navigate a transition toward sustainability?
7. How can today's relatively independent activities of research planning, monitoring, assessment, and decision support be better integrated into systems for adaptive management and societal learning?

A key step toward developing a sustainable society is the ability to portray the dynamic linkages between economic, social, and environmental systems. This is what is called systems thinking, as shown by the diagram below, constructed by my colleague Joseph Fiksel.

---

[8] Robert W. Kates, William C. Clark, Robert Corell, J. Michael Hall, Carlo C. Jaeger, Ian Lowe, James J. McCarthy, Hans Joachim Schellnhuber, Bert Bolin, Nancy M. Dickson, Sylvie Faucheux, Gilberto C. Gallopin, Arnulf Grübler, Brian Huntley, Jill Jäger, Narpat S. Jodha, Roger E. Kasperson, Akin Mabogunje, Pamela Matson, Harold Mooney, Berrien Moore III, Timothy O'Riordan, Uno Svedin, 2011, "Sustainability Science," *SCCIENCE Magazine* V 292. http://science.sciencemag.org/content/292/5517/641.full.

Systems Approach Sustainability

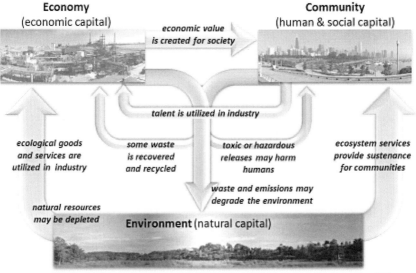

Economy
(economic capital)

economic value is created for society

Community
(human & social capital)

talent is utilized in industry

ecological goods and services are utilized in industry

some waste is recovered and recycled

toxic or hazardous releases may harm humans

ecosystem services provide sustenance for communities

waste and emissions may degrade the environment

natural resources may be depleted

Environment (natural capital)

J. Fiksel, "A Systems View of Sustainability: The Triple Value Model," *Environmental Development*, June 2012

Expanding systems thinking was one of the key strategies Paul Gilman and I used to advance sustainability.

Meeting the Future: Research Agenda and Actions Post 2003

In 2003, we embarked on two strategic paths for sustainability. The first was to create an external grants program to solicit projects across the country which we called the "laboratory for sustainable development" to demonstrate different approaches to sustainable management. The "Cooperative Network for Sustainability" (CNS) grants program began in 2004 and aimed at involving as many stakeholders as possible in specific multidisciplinary projects that demonstrated the value of sustainable management approaches.

To advance this program and drawing on Bill Reilly's historic perspective on EPA leadership, in 2004, I proposed to Paul that he send an editorial to *Science* Magazine. I did the first draft of "New EPA Focus on 'Science and Technology for Sustainability'" reiterating a forceful quote from Bill

Reilly "that EPA is at its best when it views its role as not just custodial but as cutting edge, providing leadership and prescribing answers to key environmental problems."

The editorial laid out Paul Gilman's vision for a new era of EPA research. He said, "I have come to realize that EPA's research and technology programs can be an effective force in the design and measurement of our progress toward sustainable systems." To demonstrate EPA's role, he is noting the launching of several programs including the "Collaborative Science and Technology Network for Sustainability," where EPA would fund regional-scale sustainability projects that are systems-oriented, forward-looking, and preventative.

To encourage the integration of sustainability into higher education and training, Gilman also noted a program I created called P3, which stands for People, Prosperity and Planet. The aim of this grant program was to solicit scientific and technological designs from teams of college students to address sustainability.

In the editorial Gilman made the point that we were built on EPA's extensive intramural and extramural research on industrial ecology; material flows; green chemistry and engineering; emerging technologies, and dozens of EPA policy tools and incentives to encourage and practice sustainable resource management.

He noted that "The integration of these many programs into everyday decision making can be a powerful tool for assisting states and local governments to design and measure progress toward sustainability.

This editorial is still accessible at: http://science.sciencemag.org/content/sci/304/5675/1243.5.full.pdf.

Drawing on the above, we moved ahead beginning to draft an ORD Sustainability Research Strategy. To broaden support for the Strategy, I planned a major international conference in 2005 on "Meeting the Future: A Research Agenda for Sustainability." The meeting was very successful and recommendations of the forum gave us a clear sense of future actions:

- There is no clear definition of and federal policy guidelines for defining and promoting sustainability. The role of EPA and federal government should be clearly defined.
- While undefined, sustainable development policies can have a far-reaching impact on how products are manufactured, how energy is

produced, how water is managed and virtually every other aspect of the economy. EPA and other agencies need to review existing policies and tools and assess how these and other policies can best be used to advance the goal of sustainability.

- EPA's new initiatives on stewardship and collaborative problem solving are important complements to traditional command and control approaches. These approaches reflect the changing nature of the environmental problems facing society today. Advancing these approaches through incentives and partnerships will complement and stimulate ongoing activities at state, city and local levels and in the business community.

- Traditional economic approaches are inadequate for advancing sustainability goals. Neither the use of Cost Benefit Analysis (CBA) nor existing statutory rules are an adequate framework for achieving sustainability goals. Concepts of resilience and ecosystem services are not easily reduced to monetary terms. Protecting rights and entitlement is a social and moral issue and needs to be addressed with social and political tools.

- CBA was developed for local projects (e.g. roads and bridges) and expanding the techniques to a regional, national or global scale causes problems. EPA should explore the use of deliberative methods of citizen juries and community-valuation workshops and subjective measures of well-being for the analysis of costs and benefits. These methods are new and research should be directed in this area.

- Significantly more resources and attention must be given to measuring the quality of natural ecosystems. Current information does not enable policy makers to act on conclusions about whether the systems are improving, declining or staying the same. The development of sustainability indicators is needed.

- Greater public literacy on issues related to sustainability is needed. EPA needs to communicate more with the public on sustainability-related issues.

During much of 2006 and 2007, we worked on the final strategy that went through dozens of internal drafts and external reviews. The final document aimed to advance systems thinking, complement risk assessment and move toward more sustainable operations. The strategy called for a shift by program offices toward developing sustainable water infrastructure, managing materials rather than waste, managing ecosystems and eco-services, and emphasizing green chemistry and urban sustainability (including green building design and low impact development).

EPA's external Science Advisory Board (SAB) reviewed and supported the strategy and in a letter to Steve Johnson (June 8, 2007) stated:

> "The Agency is a scientifically credible steward of environmental protection. That credibility allows the Agency to assume a substantive and visible role in sustainability research. A number of government agencies, private industry and non-governmental organizations have already endorsed and adopted environmental sustainability as a framework for environmental management. Therefore, the SAB encourages the Agency to use the opportunity that ORD's sustainability research program provides to promote and coordinate sustainability-based science and research activities across the federal and private sectors."

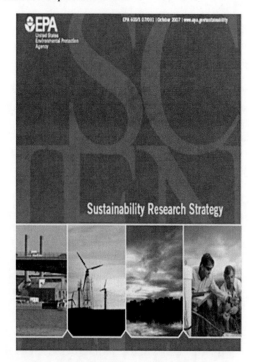

The Strategy made it clear that future needs required:

- **Systems approach:** Understanding the interconnections, resilience and vulnerabilities of natural systems, industrial systems, the built environment and human society.

- **Decision support tools:** Design and develop scientific tools and models to assist decision-makers.
- **Technologies:** Identify and develop inherently benign and less resource-intensive materials, energy sources, processes, products and systems.
- **Collaborative decision-making:** Develop an understanding of motivations for decision-making and develop approaches to collaborative problem solving.
- **Metrics and Indicators:** Develop metrics and indicators to measure and track progress toward sustainability goals, to send early warnings of potential problems to decision-makers and to highlight opportunities for improvement.

Completed in 2007, this Plan encouraged EPA's program offices to move toward developing sustainable water infrastructure, managing materials rather than waste, managing ecosystems and eco-services, and emphasizing green chemistry and urban sustainability (including green building design and low-impact development).

During this same period in January 2007, President Bush signed Executive Order (E.O.) 13423, "Strengthening Federal Environmental, Energy, and Transportation Management," which set many goals for federal agencies. This was one reason why my political colleague at EPA, Michael Brown, said "it was ok to talk about sustainability."

Advancing sustainable practices, the E.O. directed the heads of all agencies to:

"implement within the agency sustainable practices for (i) energy efficiency, greenhouse gas emissions avoidance or reduction, and petroleum products use reduction, (ii) renewable energy, including bioenergy, (iii) water conservation, (iv) acquisition, (v) pollution and waste prevention and recycling, (vi) reduction or elimination of acquisition and use of toxic or hazardous chemicals, (vii) high performance construction, lease, operation, and maintenance of buildings, (viii) vehicle fleet management, and (ix) electronic equipment management.

This Order specifies that "sustainable" means "creating and maintaining conditions, under which humans and nature can exist in productive harmony, that permit fulfilling the social, economic, and other requirements of present and future generations of Americans."

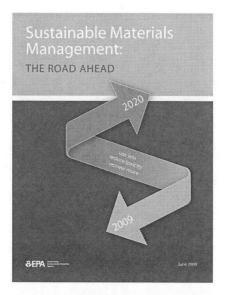

EPA's efforts to advance these concepts were outlined in an EPA report "Sustainable Materials Management: The Road Ahead," which advanced a roadmap for fulfilling human needs while using less material.

Key elements of the Report were new approaches for reducing the lifecycle impacts across the supply chain, using fewer material inputs (reduce, reuse, recycle), using less toxic and more renewable materials; and considering whether services can be substituted for products.

As we advanced our work, by the beginning of the 2010 decade it was abundantly clear to society that the world faces growing problems related to climate change, population growth, and urban development. Pressures on the earth were underscored by a famous report from the Global Footprint Network which estimated that if current trends continue, by the 2030s, we will need the equivalent of two Earths to support the world's population. This is a very important and informative group that measures the impact of human activity on the earth. Check out their web link.[9]

Parallel to our work in ORD, EPA in 2010 also created a partnership with the Department of Transportation (DOT) and the Department of Housing and Urban Development (HUD) to guide federal programs that help

---

[9] http://www.footprintnetwork.org/en/index.php.

communities to identify the resources available to support their efforts to promote sustainable communities.

The EPA's Office of Policy also expanded this, and in 2011 created the "Building Blocks for Sustainable Communities" program. This program provided technical assistance and tools to selected communities to stimulate growth and development and strengthen the local capacity to implement sustainable approaches.

NAS "Green Book"

Significant progress on advancing sustainability came with the next ORD leader, Paul Anastas, on detail from Yale University. It was his idea to ask the National Academy of Sciences (NAS) in 2010 to prepare a report on how to make sustainability operational at EPA. He was drawing on the experience of the classic NAS "red book" which back in the early 1980s advanced the concept of risk assessment for EPA. In 1983, the NAS "Risk Assessment in the Federal Government: Managing the Process," known as the "Red Book" had a strong impact on EPA. Anastas' plan was now to have a "green book."

He directed me to prepare charges to the NAS which I did in consultation with the NAS Program Director Marina Moses. We agreed the NAS panel would address:

1. What should be the operational framework for sustainability for EPA?
2. What scientific and analytical tools are needed to support the framework?
3. How can the EPA decision-making process rooted in the risk assessment/risk management paradigm be integrated into this new sustainability framework?
4. What expertise is needed to support the framework?

The NAS organized a team of scientists, chaired by the former EPA ORD Administrator Bernie Goldstein, that included scientific and business leaders including my former ORD colleague Paul Gilman, and Dow Sustainability leader Neil Hawkins.

The resulting NAS "Green Book," made significant recommendations, including going beyond the risk paradigm and adopting a sustainability framework with an emphasis on the assessment of economic, social, and environmental impacts.

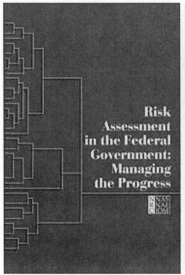
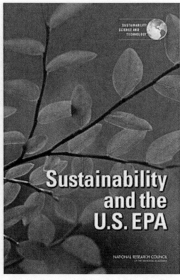

The NAS study affirmed that a "sustainability approach can strengthen EPA as an organization and position the agency as a leader in the nation's progress toward sustainability. Adopting a vision for sustainability as a goal will provide a unifying and forward-looking stimulus to the Agency."

The report specifically called for EPA to adopt a sustainability framework for decision-making, and to train the current workforce on sustainability, including the hiring of multidisciplinary professionals.

This study, completed in 2011, significantly affected EPA thinking and prompted the next Administrator, Lisa Jackson, to advance the principles of sustainability.

At the NAS release of the Green Book, left to right: Marina Moses of NAS, Scott Fulton, EPA's General Counsel, Alan Hecht and Paul Anastas. Photo by EPA.

Following the Report, Administrator Lisa Jackson (photo) launched months of "listening sessions" with EPA stakeholders to get their reactions to the recommendations. This was a good strategy to receive stakeholder feedback.

From December 2011 to May 2012, EPA held over 100 listening sessions with more than 500 participants from business, NGOs, academia, and social groups. These listening sessions conveyed a strong commitment to sustainability and support for EPA to move in that direction.

The conclusions of the listening sessions reflected a positive image of what EPA can and should do. These recommendations from stakeholders and the public are something the current Administrator should listen to and accept.

- Integrate sustainability approaches into EPA's culture and governance.
- Walk the talk and lead by example in EPA's own operations.
- Increase public discussion, actions and partnerships that create a healthier, more prosperous, equitable and sustainable society.
- Incorporate sustainability approaches into EPA rulemaking, regulatory implementation, enforcements and grant programs.
- Work with stakeholders to develop integrated regulatory/non-regulatory and cross-program strategies that address key sustainability opportunities.
- Work with other federal, state and local agencies to coordinate policies, funding, regulations, research and reporting and to achieve sustainable outcomes on a national scale.
- Improve processes for addressing the social and economic impacts that public and private environmentally related actions have on communities, especially environmental justice (EJ) communities.
- Collaborate to develop analytical and decision support tools and underlying metrics and data for use by EPA and by partners.
- Use improved metrics and indicators to evaluate progress and make improvements.

ORD Research Reorganization

Reflecting the recommendations in the NAS Green Book, EPA's Office of Research and Development in 2011 realigned its multiple research programs into six consolidated programs, all of which emphasize systems thinking and the development of sustainable solutions.

This was an accomplishment of ORD leader Paul Anastas. He said my vision for the future of ORD that the goal of sustainability was our "true north," that scientific and technological innovation is essential to the success of our mission, that we need to couple our excellence in problem assessment with an equal excellence in solving problems, and that we must act with a sense of urgency. Hence ORD was now clearly incorporating operational methods and functions to advance sustainability.

Earth Summit Rio 2012

While the above was going on, the UN prepared for the 20th anniversary of the 1992 Earth Summit again returning to Rio in 2012. The 2012 UN Conference on Sustainable Development, despite mixed reviews on its accomplishments, did result in a focused effort to develop a set of Sustainable Development Goals (SDGs), which will build upon the Millennium Development Goals and converge with the post 2015 development agenda.

The summit was a two-part event. The first week focused on hundreds of side events organized by government, business and non-governmental organizations. The second week resulted in countries negotiating a conference statement and launching new commitments. The Rio 20 plan, called "The Future We Want," contained some new goals but with limited commitments.

Overall the Conference got a mixed reaction. UN officials viewed the outcome as positive, while environmental leaders saw it as a failure. Secretary of State Clinton said it was a time to be optimistic. "A more prosperous future is within our reach, a future where all people benefit from sustainable development no matter who they are or where they live."

One positive outcome from Rio was continued leadership and growing commitment in the business and finance sector. The Conference did manage to mobilize hundreds of voluntary commitments and over 700 commitments and pledges close to 500 billion dollars to advance sustainability. Among the many commitments was DuPont's commitment of $10 billion by 2020 to research and development, and plans to launch 4,000 new products by the end of 2020 that will produce more food, enhance nutrition and improve farming sustainability worldwide.

Resilience and Sustainability

The concept of "resilience" is now a key element of present and future planning. Resilience is defined as the ability to recover from setbacks, adapt well to change, and keep going in the face of adversity. It is a critical aspect of community sustainability.

US public attention on resilience was enhanced by Super Storm Sandy (2012) which affected 24 states, including the entire eastern seaboard from Florida to Maine and west across the Appalachian Mountains to Michigan and Wisconsin. Damage was especially severe in New Jersey and New York. Overall damage in the US amounted to $71.4 billion. Super Storm Sandy was one example of the growing frequency of natural and human-induced disasters which impact cities across the US. The need for governments and communities to become more resilient was also clearly evident. The concept was also advanced by preparing for potential terroristic attacks on infrastructure and the contamination of water systems.

Since Super Storm Sandy and based on several Executive Orders, federal agencies are strongly committed to working together to advance resilient cities. An agreement between the Department of Homeland Security (DHS), the Federal Emergency Management Agency (FEMA), and the EPA is focused on providing the lessons learned for EPA, FEMA, and other federal agencies that can be used to build a stronger federal framework for mitigation planning as well as pre- and post-disaster.

As part of the reorganization of ORD, EPA's Homeland Security Research Program was created to provide the science and technology needed to effectively respond to, and recover from, intentional or accidental environmental catastrophes. Natural or manmade disasters can result in pollution that threatens human health, the environment and our economy. This research effort aims to assist communities which must be resilient to such catastrophes. Resilience requires scientific information to support good decisions.

Outside of government, one of the strongest proponents of resilient cities has been the Rockefeller Foundation which launched their 100 Resilient Cities Program reflecting three major trends: (1) rapid acceleration of urbanization, (2) impacts of climate change, and (3) recognition of the interconnectivity of all systems.

The key goals and characteristics of a resilient city are being aware of vulnerabilities, being flexible and adaptive in management, sharing information in an integrated way and ensuring coordinated actions. EPA is partnering the Rockefeller Foundation to advance systems thinking and the application of decision support tools to help cities achieve resilience.

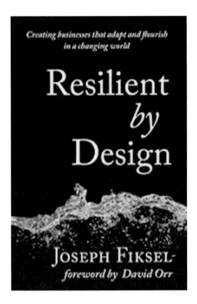

In the business world, the concept of resilience has evolved significantly. A recent book, "Resilient by Design" by my colleague Joseph Fiksel describes how businesses are grappling with the challenges of climate change and volatility in a hyper-connected, global economy.

He notes that they are paying increasing attention to their organization's resilience—the capacity to survive, adapt, and flourish in the face of turbulent change. Sudden natural disasters and unforeseen supply chain disruptions are increasingly common in the new normal. Pursuing business as usual is no longer viable, and many companies are unaware of how fragile they really are.

To cope with these challenges, management needs a new paradigm that takes an integrated view of the built environment, the ecosystems, and the social fabric in which their businesses operate.

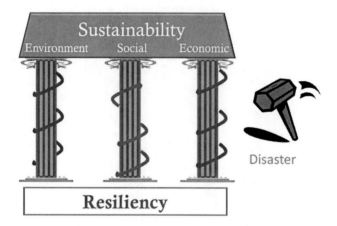

Fiksel argues that instead of merely reacting to disruptions, companies can become more resilient through the purposeful design of their facilities, supply chains, and business practices. The book provides case studies of organizations that are designing resilience into their business processes and explains how to connect with important external systems—stakeholders, communities, infrastructure, supply chains, and natural resources—and create innovative, dynamic organizations that survive and prosper under any circumstances. For EPA, a robust and resilient economy and protection of health and the environment are all components of a sustainable society. (Photo from EPA).

Hence, the concepts of resilience and sustainability are strongly linked. EPA has subsequently introduced the concept of "environmental resilience" defined as "minimizing environmental risks associated with disasters, quickly returning critical environmental and ecological services to functionality after a disaster, while applying this learning process to reduce vulnerabilities and risks to future incidents."

EPA Strategic Plan 2014-2018

After Obama was re-elected in 2012, in February 2013 Administrator Jackson left EPA and the Agency began to prepare its required Strategic Plan 2014-2018. Two additional NRC studies supported additional actions on sustainability.

The "Sustainability for the Nation" (2013) report strongly emphasized the need for integrated decision-making and identified four priority problems:

(1) the nexus of energy—food and water, (2) the need to address diverse and healthy communities, (3) enhance the resilience of the community to extreme events, and (4) promote human health and well-being.

A second NAS report "Sustainability Concepts in Decision-making: Tools and Approaches for the EPA" (2014) re-enforced the history described in this paper. The report concluded that EPA has many opportunities to further apply sustainability tools and approaches across the spectrum of its activities, and it should do so as rapidly as is practicable. Again, reflecting the emerging and interrelated challenges, the Report urged EPA to use the concepts of sustainability to strengthen systems thinking.

These two Reports came at a time of new EPA leadership. In June 2013, the Senate confirmed Gina McCarthy as the new EPA Administrator. Gina McCarthy announced five strategic goals and three cross-cutting strategies including "working toward a sustainable future."

The cross-cutting strategy "working toward a sustainable future" put strong support on systems science and an integrated approach to decision-making. This strategy specifically focused on several actions to enhance EPA's sustainability work:

- Incorporate sustainability principles into regulatory, enforcement, incentive-based, and partnership programs;
- Use available incentives, education, information, and disclosure to enhance the ability of markets to reward sustainability;
- Coordinate grants, contracts, and technical assistance to promote sustainable outcomes;
- Advance sustainability science, indicators, and tools;
- Promote new ways to encourage technology-focused innovation that supports Agency priorities for sustainability; and
- Use systems-based approaches that account for linkages between different environmental systems.

Hence 24 years after the Rio Summit, EPA was formally developing the action plans to make sustainability operational across the Agency. The recognition of integrated and systems thinking is now embedded in many regional activities. Renewed efforts are underway to ensure everyone understands what sustainability is and how it affects day to day operations.

As noted in the strategic plan 2014-2018: Sustainability isn't part of our work – **it's a guiding influence for all our work.** It has taken decades to get to this point. Now EPA can build a green and safe society, but…

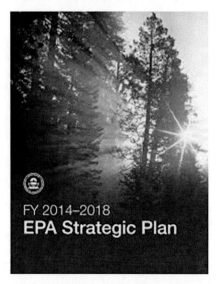

The Trump Era

As seen from this chapter, there have been a lot of steps taken to go beyond classic single media environmental laws of the 1970s to dealing with problems today in an integrated manner—protecting our health and economy today and in the future. Looking ahead, there are many roles for business and government to industry practices and technologies aiming to assure the sustainable utilization and stewardship of energy, materials, and natural resources.

What is clear today, is that the **traditional approaches are not enough.** The days of regulations or traditional approaches to risk reduction and pollution control can only go so far to deliver long-term and broad environmental quality. Today we see that business and government must collaborate to protect natural capital and assure the continued availability of critical ecosystem goods and services.

For the world today, we **need integrated management and long-term solutions.** We also need new **partnerships, incentives and constituencies.** Business and government must communicate to all stakeholders and the public emphasizing the importance of sustainability and the urgency of adopting safe and sustainable practices.

It is unfortunate that the election in 2016 has changed things considerably. The Trump Administration has no focus on sustainability. The progress of the past decades is now threatened with decline, especially if we view EPA only in its classic role as an enforcer of environmental legislation. The EPA Strategic Plan for 2018 to 2022 has nothing on resilience or sustainability.

This is a wrong approach considering the urgency of achieving a resilient and sustainable society in society today facing a growing number of megatrends.

The challenge ahead is whether the Trump Administration can deal with these problems and make America great, green and safe. One of the biggest challenges is climate change, the subject of the next set of chapters.

DEALING WITH CLIMATE CHANGE

CHAPTER FIVE

50 YEAR CHRONOLOGY OF KEY SCIENTIFIC AND POLICY EVENTS

Introduction: Climate Change is real!

Now come a few chapters on climate change. While a few people, like Senator Jim Inhofe, may view climate change as a hoax, it is real. It is ironic that the climate change debate continues today even though it is obvious that global warming has occurred and there is an increase in extreme weather events. We can no longer prevent climate change but now must adapt to it.

While writing this book, the Trump Administration released the 4th US Government Report on Climate Change, required by law and prepared by federal agencies (November 2017). This assessment concluded, that it is "extremely likely that human activities, especially emissions of greenhouse gases, are the dominant cause of the observed warming since the mid-20th century. For the warming over the last century, there is no convincing alternative explanation supported by the extent of the observational evidence."

In terms of extreme weather events, the Government Report said sixteen of the warmest years on record for the globe occurred in the last 17 years; the last three years were the warmest. In addition:

- Global average sea level has risen by about 7-8 inches since 1900, with almost half (about 3 inches) of that rise occurring since 1993.
- Global average sea levels are expected to continue to rise—by at least several inches in the next 15 years and by 1-4 feet by 2100. A rise of as much as 8 feet by 2100 cannot be ruled out.
- Heavy rainfall is increasing in intensity and frequency globally and across the United States and is expected to continue to increase.
- The rate of daily tidal flooding is accelerating in more than 25 Atlantic and Gulf Coast cities.

- Heat waves have become more frequent in the United States since the 1960s, while extreme cold temperatures and cold waves are less frequent.
- The rate of large forest fires in the western United States and Alaska has increased since the early 1980s and is projected to further increase.
- Annual trends toward earlier spring melt and reduced snowpack are already affecting water resources in the western United States.

Concurrent with the above, a new report was released by British health sciences in the medical journal *The Lancet* (October 2017). This research was part of what is called the "Lancet Countdown," which tracks progress on health and climate change and provides an independent assessment of the health effects of climate change. The Lancet Countdown is a collaboration among 24 academic institutions and intergovernmental organizations based on every continent and with representation from a wide range of disciplines.

Among the many conclusions were:

"The human symptoms of climate change are unequivocal and potentially irreversible—affecting the health of populations around the world today unequivocal and potentially irreversible"

–And,

"The delayed response to climate change over the past 25 years has jeopardized human life and livelihoods."[10]

Chronology of Actions on Climate Change

To show the long history of the debate on climate change, I have assembled a detailed chronology of classic research, scientific assessments and negotiations of climate agreements during Presidential tenures beginning with President Johnson in 1963.

As you can imagine, the literature on climate change is overwhelming. My library at home has hundreds of international and domestic reports. A scholar reading this chapter may say yes, yes, yes, I know about that!!

---

[10] This important paper is online at:
http://www.thelancet.com/pdfs/journals/lancet/PIIS0140-6736(17)32464-9.pdf.

What I am doing here is to help everyone appreciate the long efforts by scientists and policy makers to affirm that climate change is real. The more the public understands the history and the reality of climate change, the better we can prepare for the future.

My assessment is that the history shows that over the past decades there have been five stages of the climate change debate, the last being the total reality of climate change. The five are:

(1) Early recognition and fear of the potential impacts of climate change from increases in GHGs.
(2) A long period of extensive development on climate science and potential impacts of climate change.
(3) Modest advancements on international actions and agreements on reducing climate change.
(4) Intense US debate on climate change leading to a time of "climate wars."
(5) Affirmation of the reality of climate change and growing and measurable impacts on human health and the environment, as well as the economy.

Some may disagree!

The Global Warming/Climate Change Hoax
Wayne C. Weeks

"Don't you just hate it when people lie to you? I know I do. I especially dislike it when it is conspiratorial. First, we were told we were facing 'Global Warming.' When it began to seem that that was not the case, they changed the name to 'Climate Change.' Well, they can give it any name they want because it is not proved by any reasonable science. Get the real truth and the science with this book. I promise you will be better informed."

Today climate change is real and having substantial impacts on economic and social well-being. A World Meteorological Organization (WMO) report from October 2017 noted that the carbon dioxide (CO_2) levels were at the highest level in 800,000 years. According to them, the concentrations of CO_2 surged at record-breaking speed in 2016. Hence the levels of heat-trapping gas in the atmosphere are the highest in 800,000 years.

"The abrupt changes in the atmosphere witnessed in the past 70 years are without precedent," the WMO said. The WMO Secretary-General Petteri Taalas said "Without rapid cuts in CO2 and other greenhouse gas emissions, we will be heading for dangerous temperature increases by the end of this century, well above the target set by the Paris climate change agreement."

Among the many dangerous impacts of climate change are increases in extreme weather events and sea level rise. The number of heat waves has been increasing in recent years, with 2011 and 2012 experiencing almost triple the long-term average. For coastal communities, the pace of sea level rise has nearly tripled since 1990, due largely to an acceleration in the melting of ice sheets in Greenland and Antarctica. According to new studies, oceans were rising before 1990 at about 1.1 millimeters per year, or just 0.43 inches per decade. But from 1993 through 2012, the study has found that sea level is rising at 3.1 millimeters per year, or 1.22 inches per decade.[11]

Climate change is of course a global problem and requires effective actions from the top five countries releasing GHGs: China, the US, the European Union, India and Russia. GHGs emitted from any of these countries have global impacts.

Let's see how well you understand the history of climate change.

What are Greenhouse Gases?

Climate change is based on the actions of greenhouse gases (GHGs) to absorb heat. The earliest recognition of this goes back to 1824 when French mathematician Joseph Fourier was the first to propose that gases like carbon dioxide have the natural ability to trap heat within the Earth's surface atmosphere system. CO2 makes up the majority of greenhouse gas emissions, but smaller amounts of methane (CH4) and nitrous oxide (N2O) are also emitted. These gases are released during the combustion of fossil fuels, such as coal, oil, and natural gas.

Decades later, in 1896 Swedish scientist Svante Arrhenius was the first to ask whether the mean surface temperature was in any way influenced by the presence of the heat-absorbing gases in the atmosphere. He used the principles of physical chemistry to estimate the extent to which increases

---

[11]   https://www.climate.gov/news-features/understanding-climate/climate-change-global-sea-level.

in CO2 will increase the Earth's surface temperature through the greenhouse effect. He concluded that human-caused CO2 emissions, from fossil-fuel burning and other combustion processes, are large enough to cause global warming.

Then in 1938, English engineer Guy Stewart Callendar asserted that he had found a link between the rising CO2 concentrations in the atmosphere and changes in the global average temperature. He compiled measurements of temperatures from the 19th century onward and concluded that over the previous fifty years the global average land temperatures had increased and he attributed this to the increased CO2 concentration. His research and subsequent publications throughout the 1940s and 1950s led to advances in climate change science and the first direct measurement of atmospheric CO2 concentrations.

Hence as a starting point, the GHGs and global warming are a **confirmed property of science.**

Measuring CO2 in the Atmosphere and from Ice Cores

Has the amount of GHG increased in the atmosphere? In 1956, reflecting growing concern about the increase of CO2 in the atmosphere, my late colleague Charles David Keeling (1928–2005) started the process of collecting carbon dioxide samples on the peak of Mauna Loa in Hawaii .(The data from Mauna Loa are one of the most important geophysical records of changes of the Earth system.

Today the Mauna Loa station and stations around the world provide data on carbon dioxide emissions that give the clearest evidence of human influence on the atmosphere's chemistry. In 1961, Keeling produced data showing that carbon dioxide levels were rising steadily. Since then CO2 in the atmosphere has steadily risen from about 315 parts per million (ppm) in 1968 to over 380 ppm in 2005 (the year Keeling died). Keeling got the Medal of Science in 2001 (picture). Today the concentration is over 400 ppm. The increase of CO2 has led to a clear increase in global temperatures, which in turn affects the circulation system for the climate.

Photo of David Keeling from Wikimedia and Creative Commons

Historic measures of CO2 and global surface temperatures

A longer record of past changes of the atmospheric CO2 concentration has been captured by air trapped in layers of ice in Greenland and Antarctica. The ability to drill an ice core and analyze the trapped air was significantly advanced by three international scientists: Hans Oeschger (1927-1988), Willi Dansgaard (1922- 2011) and Chester Langway.

These scientists pioneered the measuring of the amount of CO2 trapped in the ancient air. In 1980 data from the ice cores in Greenland showed the cyclical nature of carbon dioxide changes in the atmosphere and the beginning of an unprecedented rise of human-caused greenhouse gases in the atmosphere. Greenland today is one of the critical areas of ice melting.

Mauna Loa Observatory, Hawaii
Monthly Average Carbon Dioxide Concentration
Data from Scripps CO2 Program Last updated October 2013
CO2 Concentration (ppm)
400
390
380
370
360
350
340
330
320
310
1960 1965 1970 1975 1980 1985 1990 1995 2000 2005 2010 2015
Year
SCRIPPS
OCEANOGRAPHY

12-Month Running Average Global Surface Temperature
Global Average Surface Temperature Change (°C)
1
0.8
0.6
0.4
0.2
0
-0.2
-0.4
-0.6
1860 1880 1900 1920 1940 1960 1980 2000 2020

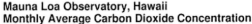

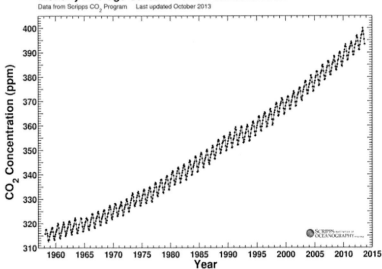

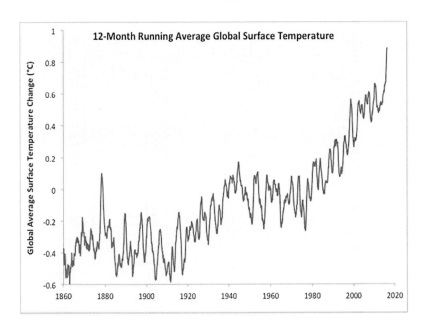

Photos of Willi Dansgaad, Chester Langway and Hans Oeschger (left), and ice-core scientists at work. Photographs by Alan Hecht August 10, 1981.

Key Science and Policy Events

As noted in my introduction, history is important. Hence, I developed the chronology of key scientific and policy actions which is summarized in the table below. It begins under the tenure of President Lyndon Johnson in 1965 and runs to 2018.

In my career, I became actively involved in climate change research in the 1970s and continued until my retirement.

What is important about this chronology is the decades of studies that converge on the fact that climate change is real. Everything in the chronology is well documented and scholarly readers can search for and access information on them from Google web links. Obviously, there are a lot of other events as well, all reinforcing the clear message—climate change is real!

Date	Key Science and Policy Event
1965	• White House Report on "Restoring the Quality of our Environment."
1969	• Moynihan memo to President Nixon identifying climate change "as a potentially serious problem."
1975	• NAS report "Understanding Climatic Change: A Program for Action."
1977	• NAS report "Energy and Climate: Studies in Geophysics."
1978	• CIA Report "Relating Climate Change to its Effects;" • Passage of the National Climate Protection Act and the Creation of the National Climate Program Office.
1979	• NAS Report "Carbon Dioxide and Climate: A Scientific Assessment;" • First World Climate Conference.
1981	• CEQ Report "Global Energy Futures and the Carbon Dioxide Problem."
1982	• WMO-ICSU Report "Physical Basis of Climate Prediction."
1983	• NAS "Climate Change Report of the Carbon Dioxide Assessment Committee;" • EPA Report "Can we Delay a Greenhouse Warming?"
1985	• Department of Energy State of the Art Scientific Assessment on Climate Change; • International Conference in Villach on "Assessment of the Role of Carbon Dioxide and of Other Greenhouse Gases in Climate Variations and Associated Impacts;" • UNEP letter to Secretary of State George Schultz on climate assessment and convention.
1987	• President Reagan established the Committee on Earth Sciences; • Congress passed and the President signed the Climate Protection Act.
1988	• Creation of the IPCC.

1989	• EPA Report to Congress: "The Potential Effect of Global Climate Change on the US;" • US-USSR Book "Prospects for Future Climate."
1990	• IPCC First Climate Assessment. • Global Change Research Act of Congress; • EPA Report to Congress "Policy Options for Stabilizing Climate;" • Second World Climate Conference (Geneva).
1991	• Congressional Office of Technology Assessment Report "Changing by Degree: Steps to Reduce Greenhouse Gases."
1992	• International agreement on the Framework Convention on Climate Change (UNFCCC); • US Global Climate Change Research Program (USGCRP); • Start of discussion of the Kyoto Agreement.
1993	• Clinton-Gore "US Climate Change Action Plan."
1995	• Second IPCC Assessment Report.
2000	• First US Global Change Research Assessment Report.
2001	• Publication of the Report on "Climate Change Impacts on the US;" • Third IPCC Assessment Report; • NAS Report "Climate Change Science."
2007	• Supreme Court affirms CO2 regulations by EPA under the Clean Air Act; • Nobel Prize for IPCC Scientists and Al Gore.
2009	• Second US Global Change Research Program Report "Global Climate Change Impacts in the US;" • Copenhagen Climate Summit; • Third World Climate Conference.
2013	• Fourth IPCC Research Report; • EPA Clean Power Plan.
2014	• Third US Global Climate Change Report "Our Changing Climate."
2015	• Paris Accord; • US Climate Action Plan.
2017	• Fourth US Climate Assessment Report; • Second Meeting of the Paris Accord.
2018	• NOAA Report Weather/Climate Disaster in 2017 cost US 300 Billion.

Lyndon B. Johnson (1963-1969): First attempt at "Restoring the Quality of the Environment"

RESTORING THE QUALITY

OF

OUR ENVIRONMENT

Report of The
Environmental Pollution Panel
President's Science Advisory Committee

THE WHITE HOUSE

NOVEMBER 1965

The issue of climate change can be easily overshadowed by other major events. In 1965 the war in Vietnam dominated public attention. An Anti-war movement began to grow and on November 13, 35,000 marched on Washington protesting about the war.

It was during this year that President Johnson was informed of the potential impact of climate change. The President's Environmental Pollution Board of his Science Advisory Committee released a report, "Restoring the Quality of our Environment" that described the impacts of both air and water pollution and climate change on the environment.

This focus on pollution occurred five years before the EPA was created. The Report said that "Carbon dioxide is being added to the earth's atmosphere by the burning of coal, oil, and natural gas at the rate of six billion tons a year. By the year 2000 there will be about 25 per cent more carbon dioxide in our atmosphere than at present. Exhausts and other releases from automobiles contribute a major share to the generation of smog."

President Johnson's reaction was "I intend to give high priority to increasing the numbers and quality of the scientists and engineers working on problems related to the control and management of pollution."[12]

The section of the Report on atmospheric carbon dioxide and climate change was written by several prominent climate scientists: Roger Revelle, Wallace Broecker, Charles Keeling, Harmon Craig, and Joseph Smagorinsky. The Report was an early warning that we "will modify the heat balance of the atmosphere to such an extent that marked changes in climate could occur."

Ten years later, one contributor to the 1965 Report, Wallace Broecker published a significant paper "Climatic Change: Are We on the Brink of a Pronounced Global Warming?" (1975). Broecker was among the first climate scientists to use simple climate models to project future global temperature changes. His paper is widely credited with coining the term "global warming."

Broecker's projected increase in CO2 is very close to reality. He projected 373 ppm in 2000 and 403 ppm in 2010 (actual values were 369 and 390 ppm, respectively).

Richard Nixon (1969-1973): Actions on Pollution and Climate Change

The issue of pollution and climate change was later addressed by President Nixon. As discussed in the previous chapters, the need to create the EPA was driven by many pollution-related events in the 1960s which spurred public attention and Congressional action. 1970 was the time of the creation of NEPA, CEQ and the EPA.

As discussed in the previous chapters NEPA had a vision of dealing with present and future problems. Dealing with climate change does reflect the emphasis on present and future generations and in September 1969, Nixon's advisor Daniel Patrick Moynihan sent a memo to President Nixon's chief of staff John Ehrlichman, **identifying climate change as a potentially serious environmental problem.** This is 1969.

---

[12] http://www.presidency.ucsb.edu/ws/?pid=27355.

He said:

> "As with so many of the more interesting environmental questions, we really don't have very satisfactory measurements of the carbon dioxide problem. On the other hand, this very clearly is a problem, and, perhaps most particularly, is one that can seize the imagination of persons normally indifferent to projects of apocalyptic change."[13]

Hence nearly 50 years ago, the issue of climate change and global warming was identified and was getting more and more global attention especially as drought in sub-Saharan Africa from 1968 to 1972 was causing widespread suffering.

Gerald Ford (1973-1974)/1974-1977) Emerging Energy Crises and Climate Change

During this Administration, the Arab Oil Embargo in 1973-1974 was a dominant economic issue impacting the US. Before resigning, President Nixon tried to end the embargo and took actions to protect US energy production. Early in his administration, President Ford said that he would not sit by and watch the nation continue to talk about an energy crisis and do nothing about it. He aimed to achieve energy independence for the US by 1985, and to regain world leadership in energy.

In his 1975 State of the Union speech, President Ford laid out his vision:

> "I have a very deep belief in America's capabilities. Within the next 10 years, my program envisions: 200 major nuclear power plants; 250 major new coal mines; 150 major coal-fired power plants; 30 major new oil refineries; 20 major new synthetic fuel plants; the drilling of many thousands of new oil wells; the insulation of 18 million homes; and the manufacturing and the sale of millions of new automobiles, trucks and buses that use much less fuel."[14]

His emphasis on coal occurs at a time when the full impact of climate change was not fully understood. This was a time, however, when the issue of climate change was getting a lot of attention from climate scientists and in 1975 several important papers on climate change were published. In addition to the work of Wallace Broecker mentioned above, two prominent government scientists (Syukuro Manabe and Richard

---

[13] https://www.nixonlibrary.gov/virtuallibrary/releases/jul10/56.pdf.
[14] http://www.nytimes.com/2007/01/05/opinion/05friedman.html.

Wetherald) developed a three-dimensional global climate model that gave a roughly accurate representation of the current climate. Doubling CO2 in the model's atmosphere gave a roughly 2°C rise in the global temperature (Manabe 1975).[15]

It was in this same year that a report from the National Academy of Science (NAS), "Understanding Climatic Change: A Program for Action" called for better understanding of climate change research.

As noted in the previous chapter the NAS is a major independent organization of scientists dealing with a wide range of complex issues. They are often asked by Congress for recommendations on a host of issues. Many NAS Reports were done on climate change as shown in the chronology.

The introduction of the 1975 NAS report declared, "Climatic change has been a subject of intellectual interest for many years. However, there are now more compelling reasons for its study: the growing awareness that our economic and social stability is profoundly influenced by climate and that man's activities themselves may be capable of influencing climate in possibly undesirable ways. The climates of the earth have always been changing, and they will doubtless continue to do so in the future. How large these future changes will be, and where and how rapidly they will occur, we do not know."

Two years later in **1977,** the NAS undertook another study "Energy and Climate: Studies in Geophysics" noting that "It has become increasingly apparent in recent years that human capacity to perturb inadvertently the global environment has outstripped our ability to anticipate the nature and extent of the impact. It is time to redress that imbalance."

The Report raised four critical questions:

1. What concentrations of carbon dioxide can be expected in the atmosphere at different times in the future, for given rates of combustion of fossil fuels?
2. What climatic changes might result from the increased atmospheric carbon dioxide?
3. What would be the consequences of such climatic changes for human societies and for the natural environment?

---

[15] "The Effects of Doubling the CO2 Concentration on the Climate of a General Circulation Model" *Journal of Atmospheric Sciences*, 32.

4. What, if any, countervailing human actions could diminish the climatic changes or mitigate their consequences?

Addressing these issues would now fall to the Carter administration.

Jimmy Carter (1977-1981) National Climate Protection Act

Photo of Congressman George Brown

In the US growing concerns about climate change led California Congressman George Brown (1920–1999) to lead the approval of the National Climate Program Act (NCPA) which he introduced and President Carter signed in 1978.

This historic and important Act created a National Climate Program Office (NCPO) and an interagency Policy Board with responsibilities to prepare a national plan and to oversee its implementation.

This important Act called for the development of a 5-year federal plan to assess the "effect of climate on the natural environment, agricultural production, energy supply and demand, land and water resources, transportation, human health, and national security."

The NCPO was a critical first step in launching interagency cooperation. It would be later replaced (in 1992) by the US Global Change Research Program (USGCRP), mandated by the Global Change Research Act of 1990 to "assist the nation and the world to understand, assess, predict, and respond to human-induced and natural processes of global change."

The NCPO was enacted with bipartisan Congressional support, noting that the "ability to anticipate natural and man-induced changes in climate would contribute to the soundness of policy decisions in the public and private sectors." The Act reflected that the "United States lacked a well-defined and coordinated program in climate-related research, monitoring, assessment of effects, and information utilization."

Congress agreed at the time that "Information regarding climate is not being fully disseminated or used, and Federal efforts have given insufficient attention to assessing and applying this information" and that the "United States lacked a well-defined and coordinated program in climate-related research, monitoring, assessment of effects, and information utilization."

The first NCPO Five Year Climate Plan of 1980 laid out the research needed across federal agencies. It is ironic that in 1980 the context for the plan's creation was extreme weather events which we are experiencing today.

In 1979 another NAS study on "Carbon Dioxide and Climate: A Scientific Assessment" also warned, "If carbon dioxide continues to increase, [we] find no reason to doubt that climate changes will result, and no reason to believe that these changes will be negligible."

This was the same year that the first

World Climate Conference (WCC) was organized. The conference, organized by the World Meteorological Organization (WMO) was chaired by the late Robert White (1923–2015) who was one of the creators of NOAA (photo).

Bob White was also instrumental in moving me from NSF to NOAA in 1981 to lead the NCPO.

He worked hard at the conference to get international consensus on a declaration that would establish a World Climate Program. White was a leader on weather and climate and served as the director of the United States Weather Bureau from 1963 to 1965, the director of the Environmental Science Services Administration from 1965 to 1970, and the first administrator of the National Oceanic and Atmospheric Administration (NOAA) from 1970 to 1977. He was the president of the National Academy of Engineering from 1983 to 1995.

The WCC called upon governments to foresee and to prevent potential man-made changes in climate that might impact the well-being of humanity. The conference's final declaration "called for global cooperation to explore the possible future course of global climate and to take this new understanding into account in planning for the future development of human society."

A major outcome of the Conference was the organization of the World Climate Research Program (WCRP) jointly organized by the WMO, the United Nations Environment Program (UNEP) and a Paris-based science group called the International Council of Scientific Unions (ICSU). They in turn organized several international workshops in 1980, 1983, and 1985; the last one being a crucial meeting in setting the stage for international negotiations of a climate agreement and the creation of the Intergovernmental Panel on Climate Change (IPCC).

Also, in the last days of the Carter administration, Gus Speth of the Council on Environmental Quality (CEQ) published a report, "Global Energy Futures and the Carbon Dioxide Problem" (1980). This report noted that back in 1800 the atmospheric concentration of CO_2 was about 290 parts per million (ppm). Since then, it has increased between 15 and 25 per cent. The Report looked ahead and said that the "analysis underscores the importance of the 2000-2020 time periods for fossil fuel use and consequently the utility of undertaking planning and action now if certain levels of atmospheric CO_2 are to be avoided."

Significant pressure both domestically and internationally were now growing on climate change and continue under the tenure of the Reagan Administration.

Ronald Reagan (1981-1989) Era of Major Advances on Climate Science

The strength of the economy is a major issue for all Presidents and unfortunately the Reagan Administration inherited an economy that was in deep decline. Nevertheless, it was during this period that there was a major focus on the climate debate. In 1982 the WMO and the ICSU issued a Report on the "Physical Basis for Climate Prediction" which identified three critical issues: (1) mechanisms governing climate variability, (2) the prediction of climate change, and (3) applying a strategy for further work.

Paralleling the international focus on climate change, several members of Congress with growing concern about the scientific uncertainty of climate change turned to the NAS to prepare another assessment. The NAS report "Climate Change Report of the Carbon Dioxide Assessment Committee" in 1983 reaffirmed the prediction of a long-term climate warming associated with increasing GHGs, but took a cautious approach toward policy.

Two days before the Changing Climate Report was released, the EPA released its first climate report, "Can We Delay a Greenhouse Warming?" The study was aimed to assess "whether specific policies aimed at limiting the use of fossils fuels would prove effective in delaying temperature increases over the next 120 years." The EPA report raised the specter of a world on a collision course between the need for energy, with coal seen as the least expensive source for meeting that need, and global warming of potentially catastrophic proportions.

Although the tone of the EPA report was more alarming than the NAS report, its policy conclusions were essentially the same, namely that no current, reasonable policy options would significantly delay or reduce the amount of warming. The only policy that would be effective was a complete ban on the use of coal and shale oil starting in 2000, but such a ban was not feasible.

Two years later in 1985, in a critical long-range planning document, UNEP called for a "convention" (i.e. international agreement) on climate change. Toward the goal of establishing a scientific basis for an agreement on climate change, they convened a scientific meeting on the "Assessment of the Role of Carbon Dioxide and of Other Greenhouse Gases in Climate Variations and Associated Impacts" in Villach, Austria.

The scientific findings of the Villach meeting were summarized by the ICSU in a report that stated that "substantial warming" would occur from a doubling of CO2, "attributable to human activities." The summary recommended a variety of specific policy actions and urged more significant steps toward international cooperation on climate change and government actions on policies concerning fossil fuel use, energy conservation and greenhouse gas emissions.

UNEP's efforts to promote a convention on climate did in turn trigger the development of the Intergovernmental Panel on Climate Change (IPCC). In response to the recommendations of the Villach report, UNEP's Executive Director Moustafa Tolba sent a letter to Reagan's Secretary of State George Schultz, urging the US to take appropriate actions. The State Department passed the letter to the NCPO where federal agencies debated future actions and ultimately came up with an agreement for an international governmental scientific assessment.

During this time, I was the head of the NCPO (from 1981 to 1989) and worked hard with the NCPO to develop a draft response to Tolba's letter. I had a colleague, Bo Döös (1922-2010) on detail from the WMO, who was especially helpful in preparing a response and proposed the idea of an "Intergovernmental Panel on the Assessment of Climate Change." This idea led to a US proposal responding to the UNEP letter for an intergovernmental "mechanism" to conduct a government-led, scientific assessment of the climate change issue.

This mechanism later became the Intergovernmental Panel on Climate Change (IPCC). The IPCC was a joint creation of two international organizations: UNEP and WMO. The creation of the IPCC and the publication of its first assessment of the impact of climate change were critical steps leading to the first international climate convention.

In 1987 Congress requested EPA to undertake two additional studies on impacts of climatic change and possible options in response to greenhouse warming. The first study ("The Potential Effect of Global Climate Change on the US") published in 1989, examined the potential effects of climate change on the US. The second one in 1990 ("Policy Options for Stabilizing Climate") examined policy options to stabilize and reduce the emissions of greenhouse gases. These Reports generated intense interagency debate because they identified the need for a broad spectrum of regulatory, fiscal, and educational measures such as increased automobile efficiency, accelerated use of renewable energy, strengthened appliance standards, and carbon taxes.

A continuing and growing focus on climate change led Congress in 1987 to pass the Global Climate Protection Act directing the President to establish a Task Force on the Global Climate to research, develop, and implement a coordinated national strategy on global climate. What Congress wanted was a US strategy on climate change. The Act also directed the EPA and the Department of State to develop policy options for dealing with greenhouse-based climate change and for coordinating international activities. This was clearly a period of building consensus on scientific evidence on the impact of climate change.

And in 1988 the IPCC was created by the WMO and UNEP. The task of the IPCC, outlined in UN General Assembly Resolution 43/53 (December 1988) was to prepare a comprehensive review and recommendations with respect to the state of knowledge of the science of climate change; the social and economic impact of climate change, and possible response strategies and elements for inclusion in a possible future international convention on climate.

By November 1988, the IPCC was fully functional and work began on preparing its first reports. I have more on this in the next chapter.

The first scientific assessment in 1990 underlined the importance of climate change as a challenge requiring international cooperation to tackle its consequences. This was a critical first step in getting international consensus on the reality of climate change and played a decisive role in leading to the creation of the United Nations Framework Convention on Climate Change (UNFCCC), which was the key international treaty to reduce global warming and cope with the consequences of climate change.

The critical steps to prepare the first report and resolve international differences are discussed in the next chapter. It is here that I played a key role in resolving differences with the then USSR.

Since then the IPCC has delivered on a regular basis the most comprehensive scientific reports about climate change produced worldwide: the Assessment Reports. The IPCC Second Assessment Report of 1995 provided important material that was drawn on by negotiators in the run-up to the adoption of the Kyoto Protocol in 1997. The Third Assessment Report came out in 2001, the Fourth in 2007 and the latest Assessment in 2014.

While all of this was going on, the Upper Midwest had the worst drought in 50 years. The NASA scientist and climate modeler James Hansen (retired 2013) testified before the Senate Energy Committee in 1988. In a bold statement, he said he was 99 per cent certain that the unusually warm, globally averaged temperatures for the 1980s could not have occurred by chance, but rather were the result of the buildup of greenhouse gases. Hansen went on to postulate that increasing the global temperature would increase the likelihood of extreme heat waves such as those occurring in 1988. This testimony heightened the public debate in the US on greenhouse warming.

George Bush (1989-1993) Launching the UN Convention on Climate Change

With an election coming up, Candidate George Bush, in a September 1988 speech in Boston said, "Those who think we're powerless to do anything about the greenhouse effect are forgetting about the White House effect. As President, I intend to do something about it."

In 1989, the US Global Change Research Program (USGCRP) began as a Presidential Initiative but was later mandated by Congress in the Global Change Research Act (GCRA) of 1990 to "assist the Nation and the world to understand, assess, predict, and respond to human-induced and natural processes of global change." The Act requires the US to develop and coordinate "a comprehensive and integrated United States research program which will assist the Nation and the world to understand, assess, predict, and respond to human-induced and natural processes of global change."

The Act mandates that every four years a report is done by the US on how climate change is affecting different regions of the country. A summary of the upcoming Fourth Report was released in August 2017 at the time of the beginning of the Trump Administration.

Results from the US Climate Review and the IPCC were critical in affirming the reality of climate change.

In 1990 the IPCC released the first assessment that provided momentum for the negotiations of the Framework Agreement on Climate Change (FACC). More discussion of this comes in the next chapter.

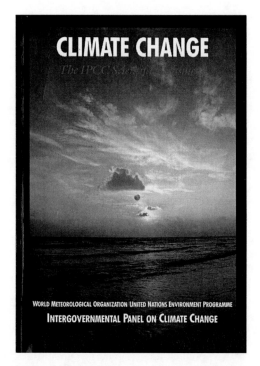

The IPCC scientific assessment also broke new ground by attempting to account for the impact of greenhouse gas on the "radiative" balance of the atmosphere by using an index—the Global Warming Potential (GWP)—that accounted for both the greenhouse effect of the gas and its lifetime in the atmosphere.

The Report concluded that "the potential serious consequences of climate change on the global environment give sufficient reasons to begin adopting response strategies that can be justified immediately even in the face of significant uncertainties."

In a 1991 summary of the IPCC Report, the UK's John Houghton (Chairman of the Working Group) said "I am confident that the Assessment and its Summary will provide the necessary firm scientific foundation for the forthcoming discussions and negotiations on the appropriate strategy for the response and actions regarding the issue of climate change.

It is thus, I believe a significant step forward in meeting what is potentially the greatest global environmental challenge facing mankind."

In December 1990, the IPCC Report was accepted by the United Nations General Assembly (UNGA) which also established the Intergovernmental Negotiating Committee (INC) to lead on developing a framework convention on climate. The UN resolution called for the completion of the negotiations of the climate convention in time for the Earth Summit planned for Rio in 1992. 1990 was also the time of the Second World Climate Conference in Geneva.

The negotiations of the United Nations Framework Convention on Climate Change (UNFCCC) began **in 1991.** It would take five subsequent negotiation sessions, ending in New York in 1992. In the negotiations, the US opposed any binding targets and timetables. The Bush administration had a strong perception that a binding commitment to "stabilize" GHG emissions could force the US to adopt policy actions with unforeseen economic consequences. Compromises in the Agreement were ultimately supported by President Bush. The UNFCCC was adopted on May 9, 1992 and would be open for signing at the Earth Summit in Rio in 1992. Two years later, it would be entered into force on 21 March 1994, after a sufficient number of countries had ratified it.

The key objective of the UNFCCC is to "stabilize greenhouse gas concentrations in the atmosphere at a level that would prevent dangerous anthropogenic interference with the climate system." The framework sets no binding limits on greenhouse gas emissions for individual countries and contained no enforcement mechanisms. Instead, the framework outlines how specific international treaties (called "protocols" or "Agreements") may be negotiated to specify further action toward the objective of the UNFCCC.

Bill Clinton (1993-2001) US Climate Change Action Plan/Negotiating the Kyoto Protocol

In support of the UNFCCC, President Clinton and Vice President Gore released in October 1993, the Climate Change Action Plan, a voluntary set of commitments to reduce the emissions of greenhouse gases to 1990 levels. The two goals of the Action Plan were to strengthen the US economy and to reduce the emissions of greenhouse gases. In the Executive Summary, President Clinton said, "We must take the lead in addressing the challenge of global warming that could make our planet and its climate less hospitable and more hostile to human life."

While the Action Plan identified over forty federal programs for possible business collaborations it did not get fully implemented. In 1993 President Bill Clinton also proposed a BTU tax on all fuel sources based on their heat content except for wind, solar, and geothermal sources. It was never adopted. The BTU tax passed the House but was rejected by the Senate.

It was during the Clinton Administration that negotiations began for the Kyoto Protocol which would be signed in 1997, but not entered into force until February 16, **2005.** During the negotiations, Vice President Al Gore introduced the concept of "cap and trade" as one way to introduce flexibility and thus reduce the costs of reducing emissions. Cap and trade is an environmental policy tool that delivers results with a mandatory cap on emissions while providing the sources of emissions with flexibility in how they comply.

While in 1998, President Clinton signed the Kyoto Protocol, he did not submit it to the Senate for advice and consent. The following administration under George Bush would pull out of the Protocol. Under Bush's tenure, the United States experienced a period of what I call "climate wars," in which conflicts centered on 1) the reality of climate science; 2) the economic impact of GHG regulations; and 3) the expanding role of EPA. This is also discussed in more detail in chapter 7.

In the year 2000, the First National Climate Assessment, "Climate Change Impacts on the United States: The Potential Consequences of Climate Variability and Change" was completed. It was formally published in 2001. This Report seriously advanced the understanding of what climate change meant for America. This assessment began a national process of research, analysis, and dialogue about the coming changes in climate, their impacts, and what Americans can do to adapt to an uncertain and continuously changing climate. This would be a struggle for the Bush Administration.

George W. Bush (2001-2009) Time of Climate Wars

During the 2000 presidential campaign, candidate George W. Bush promoted legislation to "require the mandatory reduction in the US of emissions of sulfur dioxide, nitrogen oxide, mercury and carbon dioxide from power plants." Many observers saw this as a significant departure from past Republican positions and were optimistic that a new era of environmental protection was about to begin.

Unfortunately, the campaign promise in 2000 was reversed the following March (2001) and for much of his Administration there were serious conflicts on climate change, as discussed in Chapter 7.

Of course, the Bush Administration functioned at a time of major global conflicts. It was the time of the September 11, 2001 (9/11) terrorist attacks in New York. It was also a time when the economy had a 1.6 per cent GDP growth rate. Many business leaders and Washington politicians believed that the sluggish economy should not be laden with extra tax burdens on business, especially on the energy sector. Based on such fears, there were many attacks on climate science. Such attacks stressed scientific uncertainty and attempted to discredit any scientific evidence that could support new federal legislation or regulations on carbon emissions.

This was also a time when the "Global Climate Coalition" (GCC) (1989–2001) was formed under the auspices of the National Association of Manufacturers. The GCC was the largest industry group active in promoting skeptical views on climate science and policy. They dissolved in 2001 after membership declined in the face of improved understanding of the role of greenhouse gases in climate change and of public criticism.

2001 was also the year that the White House got a response from the NAS to their request to "assist in identifying the areas in the science of climate change where there are greatest certainties and uncertainties" and an assessment of the IPCC reports. The NAS Report "Climate Change Science" did affirm that GHGs are accumulating in the Earth's atmosphere resulting from human activities, causing surface air temperatures and subsurface ocean temperatures to rise. They noted that the changes observed over the last several decades are most likely due to human activities. The Report offered no policy recommendations but did affirm the conclusions of the IPCC reports.

In the same year, 2001, the major report of the National Assessment Synthesis Team of the US Global Change Research Program was published on "Climate Change Impacts on the US: The Potential Consequences of Climate Variability and Change." This is a "landmark" report noting that "Climate science is developing rapidly and scientists are increasingly able to project some changes at the regional scale, identifying regional vulnerabilities, and assessing potential regional impacts."

The summary of this report notes that "long-term observations confirm that our climate is now changing at a rapid rate. Over the 20th century, the average annual US temperature has risen by almost 1°F (0.6°C) and precipitation has increased nationally by 5 to 10%, mostly due to increases in heavy downpours. These trends are most apparent over the past few decades. The science indicates that the warming in the 21st century will be significantly greater than in the 20th century." The full Report of over 500 pages is available at: http://agecon2.tamu.edu/people/faculty/mccarl-bruce/papers/906.pdf.

Despite progress being made on climate change, there was still political opposition. Senator Inhofe gave a speech in the Senate on September 25, 2006 saying, "I am going to speak today about the most media-hyped environmental issue of all time, global warming."

It was also at this time that the Supreme Court affirmed that the EPA has the authority to regulate CO_2 emissions from automobiles. The case resolved a conflict between several states and the federal government. President Bush did issue an Executive Order in May 2007 that directed EPA and the departments of Transportation, Energy, and Agriculture to coordinate in developing possible regulatory actions to address emissions from mobile sources contributing to global climate change. This would be a complicated process requiring EPA to assert that the carbon emissions endanger public health and welfare under the Clean Air Act.

In **2007,** the Nobel Prize was also awarded to the IPCC and Al Gore for their efforts to build up and disseminate greater knowledge about man-made climate change, and to lay the foundations for the measures that are needed to counteract such change." The award paid tribute to IPCC scientists noting that "through the scientific reports it has issued over the past two decades, the IPCC has created an ever-broader informed consensus about the connection between human activities and global warming.

Thousands of scientists and officials from over one hundred countries have collaborated to achieve greater certainty as to the scale of the warming."

A new era of climate research and summits would now begin under the Obama Administration. By the time of the next Administration, global warming was steady increasing.

Barack Obama (2009-2017) Climate Legislation and the Paris Accord

It had now been over 40 years since the first report on climate change was sent to President Johnson in 1965. In over 40 years there is now a clear consensus on the reality of climate change and its impacts on health and the environment. Further scientific data and more economic conflict follow during this Administration. In the first half of 2008, the GDP growth rate plunged into the negative range and, after rebounding slightly in 2009, settled back to an annual growth rate of less than 2 per cent. The struggling economic growth increased the hesitance in some quarters to impose further economic costs in the short run and all but killed progress on climate legislation.

During his tenure, President Obama issued dozens of executive orders and a Climate Change Action Plan (2013) aiming to reduce CO2 emissions. The Obama Administration faced many extreme weather events that were advancing the need for resilience in infrastructure development. Under the Climate Action Plan, President Obama aimed to remove policy barriers, modernize programs, and establish a short-term task force of state, local, and tribal officials to advise the federal government on key actions in support of local and state efforts to prepare for the impacts of climate change.

Supporting the Climate Action Plan, EPA proposed regulations that it projected would reduce carbon emissions from the electricity sector by 30 per cent by 2030. The new regulations were based on Section 111(d) of the Clean Air Act, which allows states to develop their own plans to meet emission targets for power plants in several ways, including upgrading plants, switching from coal to natural gas, increasing demand-side energy efficiency, and generating additional renewable energy.

On the international side, countries met again for the annual UNFCCC climate conference in Copenhagen in December 2009. This meeting had some conflict on climate actions. The final accord, drafted by the United States, China, India, Brazil and South Africa affirmed that climate change is one of the greatest challenges of the present day and that actions should be taken to keep any temperature increases below 2°C. President Obama played a key role in helping to negotiate the final agreement which did not add any legally binding commitments for reducing CO2 emissions, but did affirm that climate change is one of the world's greatest challenges and needs a strong commitment to reduce GHGs.

A major reaffirmation of the impact of climate change came in 2013 when the IPCC released their fifth assessment report and concluded that the climate system has warmed dramatically since the 1950s and affirmed with 95% to 100% confidence that society has caused most of the warming. The notion of human induced climate change was further affirmed by a scholarly data analysis of over 11,944 abstracts of papers published from 1991 to 2011. In the summary paper published by nine authors in 2013, they showed that the trend of growing consensus on human induced climate change grew steadily from 1996 to 2011.[16]

In 2014 the third US National Climate Assessment report was also completed and concluded that the global warming of the past 50 years is primarily due to human activities, predominantly the burning of fossil fuels. The Assessment affirmed several key scientific, economic, and social impacts which have been debated for decades:

- Impacts related to climate change, already evident in many sectors, are expected to become increasingly disruptive across the nation throughout this century and beyond.
- Climate change threatens human health and well-being in many ways, including through extreme weather events and wildfires, decreased air quality, and diseases transmitted by insects, food, and water.
- Climate change poses threats to indigenous peoples' health, well-being, and ways of life.
- Some extreme weather and climate events have increased in recent decades, and new and stronger evidence confirms that some of these increases are related to human activities.

---

[16] Cook, John et al., 2013, "Quantifying the consensus on anthropogenic global warming in the scientific literature," *Environ Res Letters*.

The above events led to the next round of international negotiations, the 2015 Paris Accord which aimed to keep global temperature increases below two degrees C. Ahead of the agreement, 18 countries submitted voluntary plans detailing how they will reduce their greenhouse gas pollution through to 2025 or 2030. The agreement required all countries to submit updated plans by 2020 and every five years thereafter, a time frame urged by the United States and the European Union.

In 2015 EPA also released the final rule for the Clean Power Plan. The Plan aims to reduce carbon dioxide emissions from electrical power generation by 32 per cent within twenty-five years relative to 2005 levels. The plan is focused on reducing emissions from coal-burning power plants, as well as increasing the use of renewable energy, and energy conservation.

The plan got tied up in courts for more than a year, after more than two dozen states, industry representatives and others sued the EPA. They claimed that the plan was unconstitutional, and it hadn't yet taken effect because the Supreme Court had said the plan could not be carried out while it was being argued before a lower federal court. Presidential Candidate Donald Trump along with 27 states that were already fighting the Clean Power Plan, characterized it as an overreach of federal authority—even as many of the states resisting it were already on track to meet the plan's requirements.

Donald Trump (2017) New Era of Climate Change

So now after decades of debate on climate change—and confirmation of its serious impact on society—we have a new Administration which is backing down on efforts to reduce GHG emissions.

To begin his Administration, President Donald Trump signed an executive order calling for a turning back of the Clean Power Plant Act. Trump said during the signing that the order will "eliminate federal overreach" and "start a new era of production and job creation."

He also pulled the US out of the Paris Accord. Yet in the final statement of the G20 meeting (July 2017) there was a climate and energy action plan: the G20 agreed to "jointly work to transform our energy systems into affordable, reliable, sustainable and low greenhouse gas emission energy systems as soon as feasible and consistent with the Paris Agreement."

In the US, many states are leading on efforts to reduce GHG emissions and enhance clean energy. The United States Climate Alliance has been formed as a bipartisan coalition of states that are committed to upholding the objectives of the 2015 Paris Agreement. The Alliance was formed on June 1, 2017 after the US withdrew from the Paris Accord. The Alliance members have no doubt about the impacts of climate change and are working together to further develop and strengthen their existing Climate Action Plans. Today 12 states and Puerto Rico have members, and across the country, 274 cities and counting have signed on to the Mayors National Climate Action Agenda, asserting their commitment to lowering emissions at the local level.[17]

The President also released the fourth US Climate Assessment Report, "Climate Change Special Report" prepared by 13 federal agencies. The Report concludes that "many lines of evidence demonstrate that human activities especially emissions of greenhouse gases are primarily responsible for recent observed climate change."

At the time of writing this book at the end of 2017, global emissions of carbon dioxide from fossil fuels and industry were projected to rise by about 2% compared with the preceding year. The rise in emissions followed three years of emissions that stayed relatively flat. This was the conclusion of the 2017 Global Carbon Budget, published on 13 November by the Global Carbon Project (GCP) in the journals *Nature Climate Change*, *Environmental Research Letters* and *Earth System Science Data Discussions*. The announcement comes as nations meet in Bonn, Germany, for the annual United Nations climate negotiations.

The one country contributing the most is China which accounts for 28% of global emissions. From the report mentioned above, the "return to growth in global emissions in 2017 is largely due to a return to growth in Chinese

---

[17]   http://news.nationalgeographic.com/2017/06/states-cities-usa-climate-policy-environment/.

emissions, projected to grow by 3.5% in 2017 after two years with declining emissions. The use of coal, the main fuel source in China, may rise by 3% due to stronger growth in industrial production and lower hydro-power generation due to less rainfall."

This indicates the importance of a global commitment to reduce GHG emissions.

Finally, in early 2018, NOAA released a new 2017 report on weather and climate impacts. The cost to the US was over $300 billion. NOAA notes that this was an overall record, exceeding the $215 billion in damage in 2005, the year of Hurricanes Katrina, Rita and Wilma. The year 2017 was also the third warmest year for the lower 48 states since record keeping began in 1895. A graph from the NOAA report shows the extent of damage from 1980 to 2017.

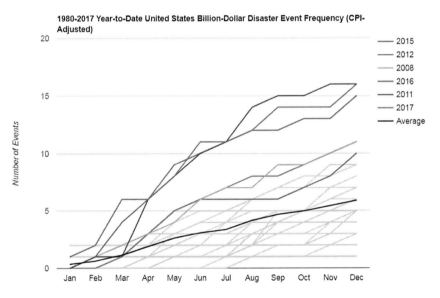

1980-2017 Year-to-Date United States Billion-Dollar Disaster Event Frequency (CPI-Adjusted)

Taken from https://www.climate.gov/news-features/blogs/beyond-data/2017-us-billion-dollar-weather-and-climate-disasters-historic-year.

So—What's Up?

This chronology shows how the science of climate change has been advanced over the past 50 years. Credit goes to the scientists who participated in the reviews of the IPCC, which was awarded the Nobel Prize in 2007, the NAS for their academic assessments, the federal agency reports and the academic scientists who have spent over 50 years investigating the cause and impacts of climate change. While there is a continued debate on climate change, it is clear now that the risks of climate change are growing and the burden on US states and cities will increase.

The final chapter of this book on megatrends gives a summary of the impacts of climate change and the increase in extreme events. In 2016, for the eighth consecutive year, severe weather events caused damages exceeding $10 billion in the US (data from the National Oceanic and Atmospheric Administration). Billions of dollars in losses are projected over the next decades.

It was estimated in a July 2017 *Science* article that the United States could incur damages worth 1.2 per cent of gross domestic product (GDP) for every one degree Fahrenheit rise in global temperature. Those damages include worsening economic inequality, heat-related deaths, agricultural declines, and even increased crime.[18]

The hard-hit States could see losses higher than 20 per cent of GDP.

In the years ahead, the challenge for both government and business is to deal with potential economic and health impacts and to adjust to the impacts of extreme weather events by building a resilient and sustainable society. Every effort must be made to reduce conflict and create more effective collaboration among governments and among government, business, and society to address the immediate impact of and future response to climate change.

Let us now go back to the first IPCC Report where I played a role in helping to finalizing the science Report.

---

[18] Hsiang, Solomon et al., 2017, "Estimating economic damage from climate change in the United States, *Science*,

CHAPTER SIX

THE IPCC FIRST REPORT AND NEGOTIATIONS OF THE FIRST CLIMATE AGREEMENT

Critical First Steps

This chapter focuses on the first IPCC assessment which was critical in launching the negotiations of an international agreement on climate change. The White House made it clear that unless the report provided a strong rationale for action, the US would not support the negotiation of an international agreement. Fortunately, it was a well-prepared science report and negotiations did begin.

As discussed in the previous chapter, creating the IPCC was the result of work by the WMO and the UNEP. Once organized came the challenge of identifying a chairman of the IPCC and its working groups. Consensus did converge on a widely respected Swedish meteorologist, Bert Bolin (15 March 1925 to 30 December 2007), to become Chair of the IPCC with representatives of Saudi Arabia and Nigeria given roles as Vice Chairs.

The IPCC has three working groups. One was on **scientific assessment**, a second was on **policy and impacts** and the third was on **response strategies**. On the question of who would lead these groups, NOAA and NASA wanted the US to chair the science group, whereas State and EPA wanted the US to chair the policy group. Following extensive international debate, John Houghton of the UK became chair of the science working group with representatives from Senegal and Brazil as co-chairs. The chair of the impact assessment group was Yuri Izrael from Russia with representatives from Australia and Japan as vice chairs. Fred Bernthal of the Department of State became chair of the response strategy working group, with representatives from Canada, China, Malta, Netherlands, and Zimbabwe as co-chairs.

By November 1988, the IPCC was fully functional and work began on the preparation of the three reports, the first of which was critical in laying the foundation for the climate convention.

My Status

In 1982, I moved from the NSF to the National Oceanographic and Atmospheric Administration (NOAA) as director of the newly established National Climate Program Office (NCPO). In this role, I was responsible for coordinating all climate-related work among twelve federal agencies. This was a tough and somewhat impossible job, exciting but fraught with bureaucratic pitfalls.

While at the NCPO, I had a role in helping to create the IPCC. Then in 1989, EPA's Administrator William K. Reilly, recruited me to the role of Deputy Assistant Administrator for International Activities.

Here I worked with Administrator Reilly in dealing with climate issues including preparing the first IPCC report and subsequently participating in the negotiations of the first climate convention. I had the pleasure of being in Sweden for the final IPCC meeting. As discussed below, it was here that I played a role in working with Russian scientists to reach a consensus on the science report.

First IPCC Report

From 1989 to August 1990, the three IPCC working groups worked hard to complete their first Reports. In 1989, Secretary of State James A. Baker III, welcomed scientists and government officials from the IPCC working group on "response strategies," which was chaired by the US.

In his first public appearance since taking office, he called for countering the dangers of global warming through reduced emissions, improved energy efficiency and reforestation. In discussing the climate-change situation, Baker was very forward looking and advocated that nations act now to deal with climate change rather than waiting "until all the uncertainties have been resolved."[19]

---

[19] See the story in the *Washington Post*
https://www.washingtonpost.com/archive/politics/1989/01/31/baker-urges-steps-on-global-warming/e0209874-c7cb-4347-996e-df54986de868/.

The three IPCC working groups worked hard for months to develop their Reports. The final IPCC meeting in Sundsvaal, Sweden was overwhelmed by intense politics. On the last night of negotiations, governments intensely debated the key recommendations of the summary report and the meeting came close to failure. What was going on was that countries were beginning to position themselves for the proposed upcoming negotiations of climate agreement.

It was here that I met with Russian colleagues to help finalize the science Report. My involvement was the result of an ongoing US-USSR Agreement. In the early 1970s the USSR had a strong interest in weather modification, geoengineering, and climate change and attracted a great deal of political attention in the US. It was President Nixon who in 1972 introduced the US -USSR scientific cooperation in oceanography and atmospheric sciences.

Much to my surprise and pleasure, I participated in the US-USSR scientific meetings for many years, first at NSF and then at NOAA, where I led one of the very active joint Working Groups (VIII) under the US-USSR Bilateral Agreement. This bilateral agreement became a key forum for addressing many climate and environmental issues.

In my work with the Russians, I had a long history of contact with the renowned Russian scientist, Mikhail Budyko (1920–2001) who was a pioneer in Russian science on climate change. Budyko and I worked together for many years and in the final hours of the Sundsvaal meeting, we met to resolve Russia's unhappiness with the Report. (Photo of me and Buidyko.) Budyko worked on developing the policy report but was not happy with the science report because it failed to include his work on paleoclimate models. The task of negotiation and resolving the problem with Budyko and the Russians fell to me.

He and I worked late into the night to reach a compromise. We achieved this by agreeing that the US and USSR would work together to assess paleoclimate reconstructions and prepare a report for our governments to consider. Thanks to the help of my colleague Mike MacCracken, we completed this report "Prospects for Future Climates; A Special US-USSR Report on Climate and Climate Change," published in 1990.

Despite the intense and frantic negotiations, countries did agree to the final report. It was clear from the intensity of the final debate that negotiations for a framework agreement on climate would not be easy. Russia was not alone in raising contentious issues. India insisted on language that put the problem of climate change squarely on the backs of industrial countries.

"You caused the problem," India said "you fix it."

With the Reports done, the United Nations General Assembly (UNGA) met in December 1990, accepted the IPCC's final report and established the Intergovernmental Negotiating Committee (INC) as the designated entity to lead the development of a framework convention on climate. The UN resolution called for the completion of the negotiations of the climate convention in time for the planned UN Conference on Environment and Development (UNCED) in Rio de Janeiro in June 1992.

President Bush accepted the IPCC Climate Report and did attend the upcoming Rio Conference to sign it. The stage was now set to begin 18 months of negotiating a framework agreement on climate change.

Scientific Assessment

The IPCC's key report was its *Scientific Assessment of Climate Change*. Based on the work of hundreds of scientists around the world, this publication critically reviewed the body of empirical evidence for global warming and the theoretical and empirical basis for climate modeling.

While the report was careful to underscore the uncertainties in both empirical and theoretical knowledge, its conclusion was critical in setting the stage for negotiating the first climate agreement.

> **"The potential serious consequences of climate change on the global environment give sufficient reasons to begin adopting response strategies that can be justified immediately even in the face of significant uncertainties."**

The IPCC scientific assessment also broke new ground by attempting to account for the impact of greenhouse gas on the "radiative" balance of the atmosphere by using an index—the Global Warming Potential (GWP) that accounted for both the greenhouse effect of the gas and its lifetime in the atmosphere.

It was evident early in the IPCC process that it was too early to achieve consensus on policy issues that were so sensitive to many countries and to agencies within governments. The response strategies section discussed policy options and criteria for establishing their priorities but made no recommendations for specific options or a timetable for their implementation. Instead, the report called for international negotiations to start as quickly as possible after the presentation of the assessment to the UN.

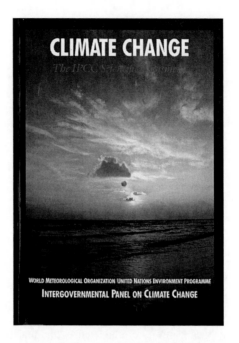

Negotiating the First Climate Agreement UNFCCC

It is February 1991 and the temperature in Washington DC broke a 108-year old record, reaching 70° F (21°C). The United States was hosting the first UN International Negotiating Committee (INC) session in Chantilly, Virginia, near Dulles airport. The meeting was subtitled: "Protection of global climate for present and future generations of mankind."

The negotiation of the climate agreement occurred under President George H. Bush who had three strong advisors who were all opposed to taking actions on climate change. This team included John Sununu, Bush's chief of staff, Richard Darman, Budget Director and Michael Boskin, chair of the President's Council of Economic Advisors.

Sununu was the former Governor of New Hampshire and was now chief of staff to President Bush. He was a particularly difficult person to deal with since he had an engineering degree and fancied himself as a knowledgeable climate scientist. During his tenure, he tried to be both a climate scientist as well as a White House manager. His office was equipped with a computer and software to run a simple climate model that could simulate changing atmospheric patterns as the levels of greenhouse gases are changed.

The fact that he worked on his computer and explored climate models became apparent to me and my colleague Robert Watson who was a British chemist working in the US on atmospheric science issues including ozone depletion, global warming and paleoclimatology. He would later become Sir Robert Watson.

Once, while Watson and I were attending an international conference in Geneva, we got a phone call from Sununu. The President's chief of staff was playing with his computer and discovered a possible error in one of the model's equations. He was calling to share the news. Watson and I looked at each other and shook our heads in disbelief.

Watson assured him that the equation was, in fact, correct!

Negotiations would end after five sessions in New York in 1992, several months before the Earth Summit in Rio meeting in June. Work during this period was intense. Building on the chronology in the previous chapter, all of this was going on in 1991

- The US National Energy Strategy is published. The plan includes a great many voluntary "green programs" developed by EPA and DOE.
- Germany reaffirmed their plan for a 25 per cent reduction in CO2 by 2000.
- Norway announced their intent to increase CO2 tax to the equivalent of $22/barrel. In Brussels, on December 13 the EC announced a strategy to limit CO2 emissions and to improve energy efficiency.
- The 12 countries of the EC agreed to create a tax on carbon and energy use.
- The US National Academy of Sciences published a report on *Policy Implications of Greenhouse Warming*. The Academy's report found that a 10 to 40 per cent reduction in greenhouse gas emissions could be achieved at low costs assuming a 1990 level of economic activity.

In 1992, the last negotiating session would occur, and at the 1992 Rio Conference over 150 countries would concur on the agreement.

Specific Commitments to Reduce GHGs

One of the earliest and longest debates in the negotiations was whether the proposed "convention" should contain specific commitments (e.g., implementation mechanisms and targets and timetables for stabilizing and reducing emissions). The idea of specific commitments was not acceptable to President Bush who was concerned about the cost of regulating greenhouse gases. Consequently, Bush was unwilling to endorse binding protocols or targets for emission reduction.

The question of the cost of regulating climate change is of course a critical issue today as well. But the cost of regulations must also be compared to the cost of dealing with the impacts of climate change. Climate change does cause an increase in extreme weather events. The US in summer 2017 faced four hurricanes ripping through Texas, the Gulf Coast and Puerto Rico with estimated damages of over $200 billion.

During the early days of negotiating a climate convention, there were mixed estimates of the costs of regulating GHGs. For example, the Congressional Budget Office published a report in 1991 suggesting that a phased approach to carbon taxes would have an impact of 1 to 2 per cent of total GNP.[20] On the other hand, a report by the Congressional Office of Technology Assessment published during the meeting in February 1991 argued that the US could reduce its CO2 emissions by 29 to 33 per cent at minimal costs within the following 25 years.[21]

At the time of the negotiations of the climate convention in 1990 and 1991, there was euphoria in Europe where Communist governments in many countries were losing power and the impact of the European Community (EC) was growing. This excitement carried over to environmental policy as many European ministers vied to make Europe the dominant influence on environmental issues. These ministers saw targets and timetables as a means of motivating their own governments (especially their trade and finance ministries) to move policies in a greener direction.

This of course was not something the Bush Administration would accept.

---

[20] "Carbon Charges as a Response to Global Warming: The Effects of Taxing Fossil Fuels." Washington, Congressional Budget Office, 1991.
[21] Office of Technology As assessment, *Changing by Degree: Steps to Reduce Greenhouse Gases*, Washington.

Final Negotiating Sessions

In early April 1992, approximately a week before the final INC negotiating session, the US released a white paper, "US Views on Climate Change." The paper was the result of difficult negotiations between EPA and DOE. The paper reanalyzed likely emission reductions from current US programs. The study suggested that the US might not be far from the goal of reducing its net emissions of CO_2 to 1990 levels by 2000—a goal called for by many INC parties—simply by undertaking energy efficiency and savings programs and other mitigation and adaptation strategies for climate change that were already underway in existing federal and state programs.

Both DOE and EPA agreed that the US could reduce its emissions by 125 to 200 million metric tons of carbon by the year 2000—within 1.5 to 6.0 per cent of stabilization. While environmentalists and other governments assumed that these results would allow the US to accept the EC's proposal for a target and timetable, senior White House officials remained unchanged in their opposition to the EC position.

In the final negotiations, the US maintained its position against binding targets and timetables. The Bush administration had a strong perception that a binding commitment to "stabilize" GHG emissions could force the US to adopt policy actions with unforeseen economic consequences.

In the end, the UK Prime Minister on several visits to the US, helped to resolve outstanding differences between the US and the EC and a final agreement was reached, **but without binding targets.**

The key goal of the UNFCCC was to stabilize greenhouse gas concentrations in the atmosphere at a level that would prevent dangerous anthropogenic interference with the climate system.

Under the convention, governments agreed to take three important steps:

1. Gather and share information on greenhouse gas emissions, national policies and best practices,
2. Launch national strategies for addressing greenhouse gas emissions and adapting to expected impacts, including developing financial and technological support to developing countries, and
3. Cooperate in preparation for mitigation measures and adaptation to the impacts of climate change.

The treaty set no mandatory limits on greenhouse gas emissions for individual nations and contained no enforcement provisions, but it did call for updates that would set mandatory emission limits.

The Agreement was also sensitive to the conflict between developed and developing countries, noting:

> "The extent to which developing country Parties will effectively implement their commitments under the Convention will depend on the effective implementation by developed country Parties of their commitments under the Convention related to financial resources and transfer of technology and will take fully into account that economic and social development and poverty eradication are the first and overriding priorities of the developing country Parties."

The UN approved the agreement in the afternoon on Saturday April 11, 1992. The following Monday, the Secretary General of the UNCED conference Maurice Strong visited the president to invite him once again to attend the Earth Summit in Rio and the President accepted. In Rio, upon signing the Climate Convention, President Bush said,

> "The Climate Convention is the first step in crucial long-term international efforts to address climate change. The international community moved with unprecedented speed in negotiating this convention and thereby beginning the response to climate change."

Photo of George Bush in Rio.

As proposed by the United States, the convention is comprehensive in scope and action-oriented. All parties must inventory all sources and sinks of greenhouse gases and establish national climate change programs.

Industrialized countries must go further, outlining in detail the programs and measures they will undertake to limit greenhouse emissions and adapt to climate change and quantify the expected results. Parties will meet on a regular basis to review and update those plans in the light of evolving scientific and economic information."[22]

These details show that negotiating actions on climate change is never easy. Even more disturbing was the ensuing climate war that followed.

---

[22] http://www.presidency.ucsb.edu/ws/?pid=21611.

CHAPTER SEVEN

THE CLIMATE WARS

It is disturbing to see so much conflict on the issue of climate change. The fear here is that actions to reduce GHG emissions have a negative impact on the economy. The coal industry would of course be hard hit.

Climate change will have diverse economic impacts on states, regions, and cities, and the national budget. There is no question that the economic impacts of climate change will occur throughout the country. All sectors of the economy—most notably agriculture, energy, and transportation—will be affected, and the infrastructures and ecosystems that afford reliable services such as water supply and water treatment will also be impacted.

The economic impact of climate change will be unevenly distributed across regions and within the economy and society. Differences in climatic, economic, and social conditions will affect our ability to adapt to climate change. Regional as well as national attention will have to focus on the risks for and vulnerabilities of the poor, the elderly, and the socially disenfranchised.

During much of the Bush and Obama Administrations, there were intense and highly politically motivated attacks on climate science and the EPA. The goal was to undermine the reality of climate science, and hence justify no political actions. It was disturbing that many key scientists were singled out in these attacks.

I had firsthand experience in these battles which I termed "climate wars" while on detail to the White House from 2001 to 2003.

Bush Administration and Climate Change

During the 2000 presidential campaign, candidate George W. Bush promoted legislation to "require the mandatory reduction in US of emissions of sulfur dioxide, nitrogen oxide, mercury and carbon dioxide from power plants." Many observers saw this as a significant departure from past Republican positions and were optimistic that a new era of environmental protection was about to begin.

Unfortunately, the campaign promise in 2000 was reversed in March (2001) following an international conference among the G-8 countries. The reversal, a surprise to the newly appointed EPA Administrator Christine Todd Whitman, (photo) was a clear indication of behind-the-scenes concerns about energy policy, economics, government regulations and their impact on the economy.

I was excited by President Bush's appointment of the former New Jersey Governor Christine Todd Whitman as the new EPA Administrator. Whitman had a strong environmental record as the Governor of New Jersey. In the months from when she first appeared at EPA until October (2001) when I went to the White House, I worked with her in preparing for several international climate meetings.

In 2001, at a meeting of the G-8 industrial countries in Trieste, Italy, Administrator Whitman announced that the US was **committed to the regulation of GHG emissions.** Whitman assured her counterparts that the US wanted a mandatory cap on CO_2 emissions.

The Joint Communiqué of this meeting expressed an international commitment to "take the lead by strengthening and implementing national programs and actions, to reduce greenhouse gas emissions, as well as to promote and disseminate environmentally sound technologies and practices and renewable energy sources."

Unfortunately, Administrator Whitman was unaware of a behind-the-scenes effort led by Senators Chuck Hagel, Jesse Helm, Larry Craig, and Pat Roberts to reverse this commitment. In a letter to the president, these senators made clear their view that the commitment was unwise.

The letter attracted the attention of Vice President Cheney who according to Barton Gellman in his book *Angler* (2008) embarked on a plan to "walk the President away from his promise."

Cheney's staff prepared a memo **"that would put the White House on record against the collective judgment of the world's climate scientists."** The memo said Bush should be nudged toward the position that the "current state of scientific knowledge about causes of and solutions to global warming is inconclusive. Therefore, it would be premature for the president to propose any specific policy or approach aimed at addressing global warming."

President Bush accepted this, and said "I do not believe, however, that the government should impose on power plants mandatory emissions reductions for carbon dioxide, which is not a 'pollutant' under the Clean Air Act."

Underlying the opposition to CO_2 regulation was the critical issue of the supposed economic impacts that would result from regulating CO_2 and who would pay for it.

The Administrator was uninformed of the reversal of her remarks and was deeply upset.

The Bush Administration's priority for economic growth was also clearly evident in all policy actions. For example, in a key chapter of the "Economic Report of the President" submitted to Congress in 2002, they focused on the cost of environmental regulations. Recognizing the significant achievement of the past decades in reducing the most obvious risks to health and the environment, the report states, "there is evidence that further improvements in air quality would improve health and reduce mortality, but these improvements might be extremely expensive."

A clear goal of the Bush Administration was to avoid any new federal legislation and regulations. This meant not allowing carbon dioxide (CO_2) to be declared a pollutant under the Clean Air Act or as an endangerment to human health. One approach to avoid this was clearly to emphasize the uncertainty in the science of climate change.

The above led to a period of climate wars aiming to undermine the reality of the science of climate change. One clear example related to EPA

Administrator Whitman is the preparation of the Agency's first Report on the Environment (RoE).

White House Attack on the EPA Report on the Environment (RoE)

While I was on detail to the White House, I had a front seat on the climate battles. The first began with the White House editing an EPA Report on the Environment.

A significant initiative of EPA Administrator Whitman was the launching in 2001 of a *Report on the Environment*. The underlying idea was to give the public a snapshot of US environment quality and to establish a set of indicators or metrics to measure improvements (or declines) over time. In launching her initiative, Governor Whitman said:

> "It is also important that we hold ourselves accountable to the American public and report to them our progress in reaching the goals we have set for ourselves. Therefore, I am directing the Agency to prepare a State of the Environment Report, which will bring together national, regional and program office indicator efforts to describe the condition of critical environmental areas and human health concerns. To perfect this report will be a multi-year process, but I believe it is important to begin the process now, and commit to continuous improvement over time. The first Report, due in fall 2002 will provide an inventory of EPA indicators, identify promising indicators that allow us to report on the environment, as well as identify data gaps and discuss the challenges we face in filling these gaps."

Such an effort is not without considerable difficulty in both collecting reliable and scientifically defensible data and in identifying appropriate metrics. Nevertheless the 2003 RoE (always identified as a draft) was a major accomplishment. Updated versions of the RoE were prepared in 2008, and again in 2014.

While launched in 2001, the RoE ran into considerable interagency difficulties and was not on schedule to be finalized in the fall of 2002. In January 2003, a frustrated EPA Chief of Staff Eileen McGinnus came to see the CEQ chairman Jim Connaughton and asked for help in finalizing the report. Several issues, including the title of the report were holding up interagency consensus.

Chairman Connaughton was supportive and directed me to help resolve the interagency disagreements.

One big issue in the RoE was the chapter on climate change. The CEQ's initial view was that such a chapter was not needed since so many other climate reports were available. I argued with Jim Connaughton that an EPA RoE without a chapter on climate change would not be credible. In the end, he agreed but made it clear that the chapter should reflect the state of knowledge as described in available public documents.

"Clearing" a Report

I want to digress for a minute on the process of "clearing a report." What this means is that all agencies or offices that have an interest in the report are given a chance to offer comments. In the end, the National Security Council (NSC) or White House resolves differences between agencies.

Modern computer technology makes this task a little more complicated. For example, given a policy paper and needing interagency review, the paper can go to dozens of staffers at different agencies all of whom can "text edit" the paper. At the end of a day I might have dozens of versions of the same paragraph often with conflicting comments in the margins.

At the NSC I dealt with this all the time and often spent a whole day on the phone calling agency staff and resolving the differences. Anything put forward by EPA always evoked opposition from other agencies.

On one touchy issue, an agency staffer told me he could not live with the EPA statement. I responded by saying, if it was expected, do I have to come over and kill him!

The White House, especially the NSC was very sensitive to the clearance process and wanted to be certain that all stakeholders had a chance to review any pending policy paper.

After our meeting with the EPA Chief of Staff, I started the process of getting interagency review and clearance on the draft chapter. The draft RoE was circulated to all federal agencies and executive offices. I resolved nearly all issues except the one on climate change.

On January 27, 2003, I got an email from staff at the Office of Science Policy and Technology (OSTP) advising that "This section should be thoroughly reviewed for content and usefulness of that content. The section 'What are the contributions to climate change' is not balanced and virtually ignores any mention of natural variability...if this cannot be balanced, it needs to be removed."

Things only began to get worse. OMB comments on the draft sent to the CEQ Chief of State Phil Cooney on March 4 said: "Phil, I don't know whether you have reviewed the Climate Section of the EPA report, but I think you and Jim need to focus on it before it goes final. Even though the information is generally not new, I suspect this will generate negative press coverage."

I worked with EPA and CEQ to try to resolve all concerns about the tone and conclusions of the chapter. On a typical day one of my EPA colleagues from ORD, Peter Preuss, who was managing the process at EPA would yell at me to "get CEQ off their back," while Chief of Staff Cooney would yell at me to "Get EPA in line."

White House Editing

In the arguments between EPA and CEQ, EPA was generally right because CEQ was trying to overplay the uncertainty of results. This was very clear to me when one morning Chief of Staff Phil Concy brought me a controversial (and scientifically dubious) science paper and asked me to include an illustration in the paper in the EPA report.

This paper, written by Willie Soon and Sallie Baliunas (January 31, 2003) contradicted published accounts of historic climate trends. The paper concluded "that the 20th century is probably not the warmest nor a uniquely extreme climatic period of the last millennium."

I quickly canvassed the scientific community on the paper and got strong rebuttals and tried to push back on Phil. I said that the EPA would not reference such a controversial paper.

Later, 13 of the authors of papers cited in the paper refuted the interpretation of their work and NASA climate scientists in a public testimony said the paper "contradicted "thousands of papers that go into a document like the IPCC report."

Ultimately, the controversy over this paper resulted in the resignation of half of the editors of the journal and an admission by its publisher that the paper should not have been published as it was.

In dealing with the climate reviews, it was clear to me that CEQ chief of staff Cooney was under pressure from others in the White House who wanted nothing in the RoE that could be used to support justifying regulations of greenhouse gases.

Four versions of the chapter went back and forth between CEQ and EPA. CEQ was clearly frustrated by the process and finally gave me a final version (April 2003) with instructions to tell EPA "to take it or leave it."

On May 23, 2003 after several days of internal EPA discussions, EPA staff called me and reported that EPA Administrator Whitman had yanked the climate chapter from the report. What Governor Whitman said, in effect, was that the chapter—as edited—would diminish EPA's credibility as an environmental agency. The benefits of removing the chapter according to the EPA staff advising Governor Whitman "were that it would provide little content for attacks on EPA's science and that it may be the only way to meet White House and EPA needs."

While politics may dominate much of our lives, principles must also be protected and in this case, much to her credit Governor Whitman put science above politics and protected the integrity of EPA. When I told Phil Cooney that the chapter had been deleted, he said "it shouldn't have been there in the first place."

The White House's editing of the RoE was exposed to the public in 2003. Phil Cooney's significant edits to the final version of the EPA Report were leaked to *The New York Times* (without citing him). On June 9, 2003 the paper published a feature story about White House censorship of the EPA RoE.

While *The Times* had copies of the text before and after editing, they were unable to attribute the editing to any single person and I did not reveal the source of the changes. It was not clear who leaked evidence of the edits to *The Times*, but it was likely someone at EPA.

Who did do the major editing would become public two years later when the House Oversight Committee held hearings on science editing during the Bush Administration on June 8, 2005; a similar incident of a NOAA report heavily edited by Phillip Cooney was reported in *The New York Times* with reproductions of his actual handwritten edits. This exposure had quick and severe consequences. Two days later, Phillip Cooney resigned from CEQ and quickly joined Exxon Mobil.

An Editor in the White House

Handwritten revisions and comments by Philip A. Cooney, chief of staff for the White House Council on Environmental Quality, appear on two draft reports by the Climate Change Science Program and the Subcommittee on Global Change Research. Mr. Cooney's changes were incorporated into later versions of each document, shown below with revisions in bold.

"STRATEGIC PLAN FOR THE U.S. CLIMATE CHANGE SCIENCE PROGRAM," DRAFT TEXT, OCT. 2002

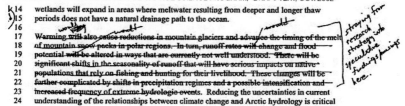

```
14   wetlands will expand in areas where meltwater resulting from deeper and longer thaw
15   periods does not have a natural drainage path to the ocean.
16
17   Warming will also cause reductions in mountain glaciers and advance the timing of the melt
18   of mountain snow packs in polar regions.  In turn, runoff rates will change and flood
19   potential will be altered in ways that are currently not well understood.  There will be
20   significant shifts in the seasonality of runoff that will have serious impacts on native
21   populations that rely on fishing and hunting for their livelihood.  These changes will be
22   further complicated by shifts in precipitation regimes and a possible intensification and
23   increased frequency of extreme hydrologic events.  Reducing the uncertainties in current
24   understanding of the relationships between climate change and Arctic hydrology is critical
```

PUBLIC REVIEW DRAFT, NOV. 2002
Warming **could** also **lead to changes in the water cycle in polar regions.** Reducing the uncertainties ...

FINAL REPORT, JULY 2003
The paragraph does not appear in the final report.

"OUR CHANGING PLANET," DRAFT TEXT, OCT. 2002

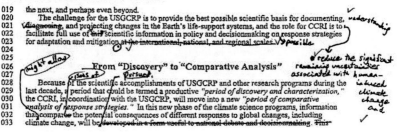

```
019   the next, and perhaps even beyond.
020       The challenge for the USGCRP is to provide the best possible scientific basis for documenting,
021   diagnosing, and projecting changes in the Earth's life-support systems, and the role for CCRI is to
022   facilitate full use of this scientific information in policy and decisionmaking on response strategies
023   for adaptation and mitigation at the international, national, and regional scales.
024
025
026   ——— From "Discovery" to "Comparative Analysis"
027
028       Because of the scientific accomplishments of USGCRP and other research programs during the
029   last decade, a period that could be termed a productive "period of discovery and characterization,"
030   the CCRI, in coordination with the USGCRP, will move into a new "period of comparative
031   analysis of response strategies."  In this new phase of the climate science programs, information
032   that compare the potential consequences of different responses to global changes, including
033   climate change, will be developed in a form useful to national debate and decisionmaking.  This
```

FINAL REPORT, 2003
The challenge for the USGCRP is to provide the best possible scientific basis for documenting, **understanding,** and projecting changes in the Earth's life-support systems, and the role for CCRI is to **reduce the significant remaining uncertainties associated with human-induced climate change and** facilitate full use of scientific information in policy and decisionmaking on **possible** response strategies for adaptation and mitigation.

Released Monday December 13, 2007

UNITED STATES HOUSE OF REPRESENTATIVES
COMMITTEE ON OVERSIGHT AND GOVERNMENT REFORM
DECEMBER 2007

POLITICAL INTERFERENCE WITH CLIMATE CHANGE SCIENCE UNDER THE BUSH ADMINISTRATION

The summary of the Bush Administration's attack on climate science was outlined in a Report from the House Committee on Oversight and Government Reform (2007) entitled "Political Interference with Climate Change Science under the Bush Administration." This Report reaffirmed that the "basic science of climate change has been well understood for many years."

It cited the IPCC Report, noting that the third Report (2001) found that "there is new and stronger evidence that most of the warming observed over the last 50 years is attributable to human activities."

This Report concluded that "the Bush Administration has engaged in a systematic effort to manipulate climate change science and mislead policymakers and the public about the dangers of global warming."[23]

Hockey Stick Attack

On the international scene, one of the biggest attacks on climate science was the science of the IPCC Reports. The battle of the "hockey sticks" began in 2001 when the IPCC prepared their third assessment concluding that it was "likely" (which it defined as a probability greater than 66 per cent) that climate change was caused by human activities, and one diagram in the report triggered intense reaction.

---

[23]   http://earthjustice.org/sites/default/files/library/reports/house-of-representative-2007-majority-report-on-climate-change-science.pdf.

This report drew on data from a 1998 publication by climate scientists Michael Mann, Raymond Bradley, and Malcom Hughes (MBH98) that reconstructed temperature patterns over the past 1000 years. The controversial graph depicted a sharp rise in temperatures over the past 100 years, which the authors attributed to human activity. The graph with its "hockey sticks" pattern was a key piece of supporting evidence in the 2001 IPCC report. This report came under serious attack; deniers of climate change aimed to dispute any claim of human-induced climate change and hence any need for legislation. Two years later, Mann testified before Congress that: "It is the consensus of the climate research community that the anomalous warmth of the late 20th century cannot be explained by natural factors, but instead indicates significant anthropogenic, that is human influences."

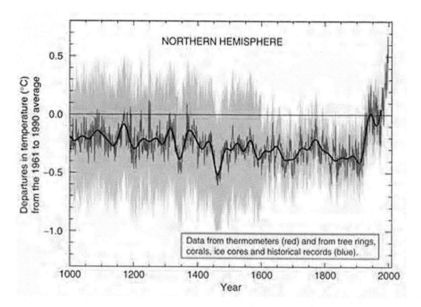

The hockey stick diagram became an element of the climate war when in June 2003, Representative Joe Barton of Texas, the Republican chairman of the Subcommittee on Oversight and Investigations, requested that Mann provide responses to eight detailed questions related to his credentials and past work.

Then in 2012, the Attorney General of Virginia, Ken Cuccinelli (who later ran for Governor) launched an investigation of Mann's research while he was at the University of Virginia, something Virginia scientists considered as a threat to academic freedom.

You can read more of the details of this and the subsequent political attacks on Michael Mann in his 2012 book "The Hockey Stick and the Climate Wars."

The Subcommittee ultimately asked the National Academy of Science (NAS) to review the issue and they formed a committee of 12 scientists to assess the main areas of uncertainty, and the principal methodologies used. The NAS report appeased both sides of the debate acknowledging deficiencies in the analysis but reaffirming the results that climate studies rely on and the quality and transparency of analyses used to support the IPCC assessment.

Considering that the essence of the scientific process is peer review and the reproduction of results, why was this paper an issue for a Congressional oversight subcommittee? Who or what was the real focus of this debate?

I saw two political objectives that underlined this debate. The first was to dispute any claim of human-induced climate change and hence any need for legislation. The second was to challenge the IPCC process and its current and future credibility by showing it relied on flawed published papers. Fortunately, the IPCC has long survived and was honored by the Nobel Prize.

In 2001, the IPCC assessment scientists concluded that it was "likely" (which it defined as with a greater than 66 per cent probability) that climate change was caused by human activities. Six years later, the 2007 report raised the probability of human influences on climate to "very likely" (indicating a probability greater than 90 per cent) and detectable in observational records.

This stronger conclusion reflected a great deal of scientific progress made over the intervening years, both in direct observations of the impacts of climate change, and in computer modeling. Nearly all scientists have concluded that current trends could not be explained without including human-related increases in greenhouse gases. While the 2007 report strengthened the consensus among most scientists and governments, a number of critics argued either that the report was too conservative or too alarming. Today, the IPCC has confirmed that man-induced climate change is in fact a reality.

CO2 is Good for You!

During President Obama's first term, the sagging US economy and global economic recession further heightened the climate wars. In the first half of 2008, the GDP growth rate plunged into the negative range and, after rebounding slightly in 2009, it settled back to an annual growth rate of less than 2 per cent. The struggling economic growth increased the hesitance in some quarters to impose further economic costs in the short run and all but killed progress on climate legislation and international agreement while the deep recession continued; this was evident from the UN-organized climate summit in Copenhagen in December 2009 and again in December 2010 during the Cancun climate negotiations.

Republicans continue to argue that the science of climate change does not justify any action. One Congressman, Kevin Brady (R-Tex.), who led the House Republicans on the Joint Economic Committee, said that the Copenhagen Conference failed because countries large and small fear the loss of economic prosperity that will accompany these arbitrary and scientifically questionable limits on carbon, "and that a growing number of people around the world are reluctant to pay devastatingly higher fuel costs as part of an unproven experiment that will not likely change the natural cooling and heating cycles of the earth."

At the same time, a group was formed, "CO2 is Green," and began campaigns to advance a concept that increases in CO2 were good, not bad.

This organization argued against proposed actions to mitigate global warming. They purchased ads in major newspapers, such as the *Washington Post*, as well as television ads, arguing that proposed measures to reduce carbon dioxide emissions would have deleterious economic effects. They even argued that increasing the levels of atmospheric carbon dioxide would have positive environmental effects. In a *Washington Post* story in February 2009, they said "higher CO2 levels than we have today would help the Earth's ecosystems."

C O$_2$ I S   G R E E N
More CO2 Results in a Greener Earth

The "CO$_2$ is Green" web site in 2009 made the claim that "there are regulators and some in Congress who want to pass laws that limit the amount of CO$_2$ produced with their claims that CO$_2$ is a pollutant. That is a myth and is absolutely false. Not only is there no scientific evidence that CO$_2$ is a pollutant, higher CO$_2$ concentrations actually help ecosystems support more plant and animal life."

Attacks like this are very disturbing considering the long history of the study on the impacts of GHGs in affecting climate change.

While climate change is real, we are again today in another era of climate wars. At EPA, the Administrator has removed dozens of online websites dedicated to helping local governments address climate change, part of an apparent effort by the agency to play down the threat of global warming.

A *New York Times* story (October 20, 2017) stated "A new analysis made public on Friday found that an EPA website has been scrubbed of scores of links to materials to help local officials prepare for a world of rising temperatures and more severe storms." Among the deleted materials are those detailing the risks of climate change and the different approaches states are taking to curb GHG emissions.

Today, climate change is one of the many megatrends impacting society that challenge us to create a green and safe society. Deleting web sites will in no way prevent more change from coming.

Let's look at the major trends impacting society.

PAST PRESENT AND FUTURE

CHAPTER EIGHT

RESPONDING TO MEGA TRENDS AND CLIMATE CHANGE FOR A RESILIENT AND SUSTAINABLE SOCIETY AND MAKING AMERICA GREEN AND SAFE

We come now to the final chapter. We need to ask ourselves, what are the growing pressures on society and what actions must we take to build a resilient and sustainable society? While the debate on climate change may continue, the impacts are real and communities, cities and states need to be ready to respond. In 2020 EPA will celebrate its 50th anniversary and since its creation it has been effective in identifying critical environmental and health problems and designing effective ways to treat them. Science at EPA is a critical step in dealing with the challenges facing society. For both business and government, critical steps are needed to make America Green and Safe.

The World in 2020

In the world today, the most obvious sources of pollution are well under control. US cities do face one classic problem, related to waste disposal and the creation of superfund sites. Over 1300 of these hazardous waste sites, scattered across the country, result from the accumulation of toxic chemicals from factories and landfills which have been dumped for decades, polluting the surrounding soil, water and air. EPA's Superfund program is responsible for cleaning up these sites and responding to environmental emergencies, oil spills and natural disasters.

The Administration under President Trump has made this a priority for EPA, one positive action in a sea of many negative ones. Under the strategic plan for 2018-2022, EPA aims to "improve the health and livelihood of all Americans by cleaning up and returning land to productive use, preventing contamination, and responding to emergencies. Challenging and complex environmental problems persist at many contaminated properties, including contaminated soil, sediment, surface water, and groundwater that can cause human health concerns."

Toward this goal one of the top priorities is progress on Superfund sites. EPA has identified 42 recommendations to streamline and improve the Superfund process. EPA will collaborate with other federal agencies, industry, states, tribes, and local communities to enhance the livability and economic vitality of neighborhoods. Recognizing the modern role for EPA, the actions of the Strategic plan are "guided by scientific data, tools, and research that inform decisions on addressing contaminated properties and preparing for and addressing emerging contaminants."

While this is a classic and unmet problem, a variety of new problems or megatrends are threatening our health and safety. A megatrend is a long-term change that affects governments, societies and economies permanently over a long period of time. A number of global megatrends include population growth, especially in cities, increases in extreme events and natural disasters, growing environmental and health impacts due to climate change, infrastructure decline, and land use changes.

In the world today, the government and business world must work together to respond to these megatrends in a way that ensures a resilient and sustainable society. The answer goes beyond existing regulations. What is needed are collaborative efforts on innovation and science and integrated systems management.

The impact of these megatrends has been described in several very important recent reports.

A 2015 Report from the NSF (*America's Future: Environmental Research and Education for a Thriving Century: A 10-year Outlook*) noted that society today was "experiencing a time in which human society and technology are **increasing the pace and rate of environmental change in ways for which no precedent exists, and which have significant potential consequences."**

This is driven by the fact that the world population is expected to increase by 38%, from 6.9 billion in 2010 to 9.7 billion in 2050. Population increase will put significant pressure on water, energy, and food resources. According to the International Union for Conservation of Nature (IUCN), "By 2050, a global population of 9 billion will increase water demands by 55 per cent, energy needs by 80 per cent, and food demands by 60 per cent."[24]

GLOBAL TRENDS
PARADOX OF
PROGRESS

A publication of the National Intelligence Council

A second report in 2017 from the National Intelligence Council (NIC), "Global Trends Paradox of Progress," outlined several stresses currently threatening our health, economic prosperity, and social well-being.

The NIC provides the Central Intelligence Agency with a long-term strategic analysis aiming to promote a secure and safe world. They are an expert group is looking ahead at future stresses.

In this Report, they noted that nearly all of the Earth's systems are undergoing natural and human-induced stresses "**outpacing national and international environmental protection efforts.**"

The Report underscored the need for an **integrated approach to management** noting that "Institutions overseeing single sectors will increasingly struggle to address the complex interdependencies of water, food, energy, land, health, infrastructure, and labor." The NIC Report reinforces the need to go beyond single media management, especially in cities which are key responders to megatrends.

A third study strongly supporting this came from the UN Global Environmental Outlook (GEO) 2016 report noting that the "environmental change sweeping the world is occurring at a **faster pace than previously thought, making it imperative that governments act now to reverse**

---

[24] http://dupress.com/articles/water-energy-food-nexus/.

the damage being done to the planet."

And, from the business world, the financial company KPMG, in their 2030 analysis of megatrends notes that the combined pressures of population growth, economic growth and climate change are all **interrelated in placing increased stress on essential natural resources (including water, food, arable land and energy).**

Hence it is crucial to advance a systems approach to environmental management and to do so in a timely manner.

Grouping of Megatrends

Looking ahead, these are the problems we face that impact the three pillars of sustainability:

- Population change, urban population growth/human health and safety/disadvantaged communities;
- Increase in disasters and severe events/resilient infrastructure;
- Climate adaptation/mega droughts/sea level rise;
- Aging water infrastructure/water usage/energy-water-food nexus;
- Land loss to urban development/ecosystem decline and continued resource use and business sector concern on the availability of future resources.

Trend	Data
 **Population Growth and Growing Demands for food, energy and water**	According to the UN, the current world population of 7.3 billion is expected to reach 8.5 billion by 2030, 9.7 billion in 2050 and 11.2 billion in 2100. Since 2008, for the first time in human history, more people now live in urban areas than in rural areas, and the pace of urbanization continues to increase. Globally, urban populations are expected to double by 2050, to 6.2 billion. It is estimated that a population of 9 billion by 2030 will have an increased demand for 50% more energy, 40% more water and 35% more food needs.

 **Increase in extreme events**	Climate change is a key factor in increasing the number of extreme weather events. Between 2004 and 2014, natural disasters caused $1.4 trillion in damage globally, affecting 1.7 billion people and resulting in the death of 700,000 people. The United States experienced more disasters over this period than any other country except China, at a cost of $443 billion in damages—winning the dubious prize for the most disaster damages, and representing close to a third of total global losses.[25] The 2015 UN Global Assessment Report predicts that disasters are expected to cost the global community up to $300 billion annually in the coming decades.
 **Impacts of Climate Change**	Climate change is already having substantial impacts on economic and social well-being and can get worse as greenhouses gases increase in the atmosphere. The latest US Climate Assessment makes it clear that there will be a strong economic impact and threats to human health. Severe droughts in the western US over the past decade have resulted in the driest conditions in 800 years. Heat waves have become more frequent and intense, with 2011 and 2012 experiencing almost triple the long-term average. At the same time, intense rainfall will continue to hit the Northeast more frequently. The health-related problems caused by air and water pollution are exacerbated by climate change; for example, it is projected that air pollution and airborne allergens will likely increase, worsening allergy and asthma conditions. Future ozone-related human health impacts attributable to climate change are projected to lead to hundreds of thousands of premature deaths, hospital admissions, and cases of acute respiratory diseases.

---

[25] "The Economic and Human Impact of Disasters in the last 10 years," United Nations Office for Disaster Risk Reduction, www.flickr.com/photos/isdr/16111599814.

	Summer extreme heat is expected to cause an increase in the number of premature deaths, from thousands to tens of thousands, which will outpace projected decreases in deaths from extreme cold. Sea level rise affecting coastal communities. Coastal counties comprise only 17 per cent of the nation's land area but contain 52 per cent of the US population which keeps on growing.[26] The insured value of property along the Atlantic and Gulf coasts rose by nearly 50 per cent from 2004 to 2012, from $7.2 trillion to $10.6 trillion.
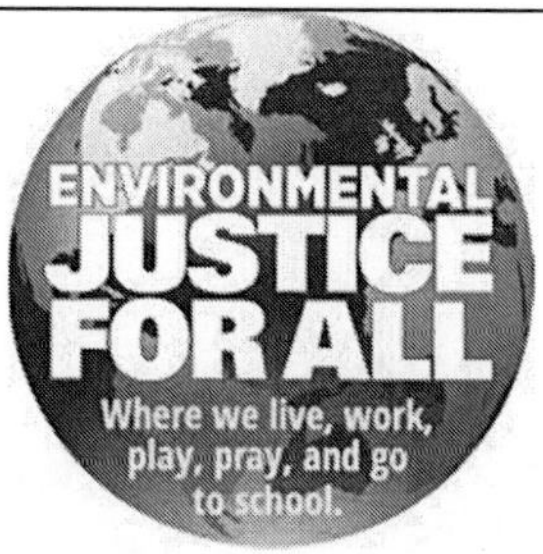ENVIRONMENTAL JUSTICE FOR ALL Where we live, work, play, pray, and go to school. **Human Vulnerability and Impacts on disadvantaged communities**	The US population is growing, aging, and diversifying. It is projected to grow by more than 60 million over the next 25 years, and the percentage of the population over the age of 65 in the US is expected to increase from 15 per cent in 2014 to 22 per cent in 2040.[27] In the United States, poverty rates have been growing; savings rates have been declining; and, disasters are disproportionately affecting the poor. Munich Re, a large insurance company, has estimated that half of total economic losses from a disaster come from uninsured losses.[28] Economically disadvantaged individuals and communities are more vulnerable to natural hazards. EPA has prepared a 2020 "Environmental Justice Action Plan" to help disadvantaged communities achieve a healthier, cleaner, and more sustainable society. The Plan was developed based on stakeholder input representing present and future environmental challenges facing American communities. It

[26] "State of the Coast: National Coastal Population Report, Population Trends from 1970 to 2020," National Oceanic and Atmospheric Administration, 2013.
[27] "Projections of the Size and Composition of the US Population: 2014 to 2060," US Census Bureau, March 2015.
[28] "Disasters in North America," Munich Re, 2012, http://www.munichre.com/en/media-relations/publications/press-releases/2012/2012-10-17-press-release/index.html.

	emphasizes the importance of infrastructure planning and design for all economic sectors and the application of tools and approaches for building resilient and sustainable cities.
 **Infrastructure Needs**	It is now clear that urban infrastructure is in serious decline. By 2030, as noted by the Rockefeller Foundation, approximately 75% of US infrastructure will either need to be renovated or built from scratch. The "Build America" program—jointly launched by the White House and the Rockefeller Foundation—encourages a forward-thinking approach to infrastructure planning and investment. It enables the Federal government to partner with local and state governments as well as the private sector to create infrastructures that are resilient to disasters and disruptions. The required investment for underground drinking water infrastructure alone is estimated to be more than $1 trillion nationwide over the next 25 years, assuming that pipes are replaced at the end of their service lives and systems are expanded to serve growing populations.
Land use change and the growing eco footprint	Driven by global population growth and associated demands for food and energy, as well as evolving consumption patterns, the pressure on the Earth's ecosystems is continuously increasing. Despite some positive developments, such as a recent reduction in the rates of tropical deforestation, global biodiversity loss and ecosystem degradation are projected to increase. The internationally-recognized Global Footprint Network has estimated that if current trends continue, by the 2030s, we will need the equivalent of two Earths to support the world's population.

Impact on Cities

Today, more than ever, cities are major centers for economic, social and environmental problems. They are now already facing serious problems resulting from increases in extreme weather and climate events such as extended droughts, extreme heat days and flooding which are seriously impacting human health and economic growth.

It is now projected that in the decades ahead, droughts in the US Southwest and Central Plains could be drier and longer than drought conditions seen in those regions during the last 1,000 years. It is also projected that rising sea levels could leave nearly 2 million US homes inundated by 2100, a fate that would displace millions of people and result in property losses totaling hundreds of billions of dollars. And in the decades ahead, cities and states will also face increased costs due to natural and manmade disasters.

In 2015 the UN Global Assessment Report on Disaster Risk Reduction predicted that disasters are expected to cost global communities up to $300 billion annually in the coming decades. Cities must also deal with increasing health, economic and social problems, especially in disadvantaged communities.

PATHWAYS TO URBAN SUSTAINABILITY
CHALLENGES AND OPPORTUNITIES FOR THE UNITED STATES

The link of social issues to sustainability has been strongly emphasized by a 2016 NAS report "Pathways to Sustainable Communities."

This new Report, which emphasizes the importance of dealing with megatrends, draws on lessons learned from several cities including Los Angeles, NY, Vancouver, Philadelphia, Pittsburgh, Chattanooga, Cedar Rapids, Grand Rapids and Flint.

Ten findings and recommendations are made including encouraging cities to develop sustainability plans that recognize the synergies among environmental, economic, and social policies and to take advantage of those synergies to advance systems approaches to management.

Looking ahead, the Report makes one very important recommendation for dealing with the changing nature of problems today: "Urban leaders and planners should be cognizant of the rapid pace of factors working against sustainability and should prioritize sustainability initiatives with an appropriate sense of urgency to yield significant progress toward urban sustainability."

The publication is timely as EPA is planning future actions on urban communities. A priority of EPA research today is to advance sustainable and healthy communities by engaging local citizens, developing tools and approaches to support decision-makers, identifying indicators and metrics, and advancing social equity and environmental justice.

These recommendations reaffirm goals being advanced by the Smart Cities Council which has emphasized that there is an urgency for cities to make critical decisions in the next 10 years in order to effectively deal with all problems. The same is true for EPA as we prepare our roadmap for the Agency's 50th anniversary in 2020. Population growth, increases in extreme weather events and natural disasters, environmental and health impacts due to climate change, infrastructure decline, and land use changes are strongly impacting our economic, social, and environmental well-being.

Today it is abundantly clear that we must be out front on issues and aim to build a resilient and sustainable society.

World Focus on Megatrends

World attention on these megatrends is clearly illustrated by the United Nations which in 2015 adopted the UN Sustainable Development Goals

(SDGs). The 17 goals have 169 specific targets and 230 individual indicators to monitor the goals and actions. The links between these goals and the megatrends are shown in the table below.

The UNSDGs have attracted considerable attention from the business world. For example, the Global Reporting Initiative (GRI), the United Nations Global Compact, and the WBCSD have joined forces in mobilizing the private sector to play a key role in achieving these goals. They assert that over the next decade responsible businesses can provide an extraordinary boost in realizing the UNSDGs through innovation and investment.

Implementation of these goals has not attracted US government attention. Yet action on these goals can reduce the impact of the megatrends. It is here that business-government cooperation on achieving the UNSDGs can advance a resilient and sustainable society.

Here I relate the goals to the megatrends discussed above:

Megatrend	Related UNSDGs
Population Growth, Communities and Consumption	Goal 1. End poverty in all its forms everywhere Goal 2. End hunger, achieve food security and improved nutrition and promote sustainable agriculture Goal 6: Ensure access to water and sanitation for all
Increase in Extreme Events and Natural Disaster	Goal 9. Build resilient infrastructure, promote inclusive and sustainable industrialization and foster innovation Goal 11. Make cities and human settlements inclusive, safe, resilient and sustainable
Climate Change	Goal 7. Ensure access to affordable, reliable, sustainable and modern energy for all Goal 13. Take urgent action to combat climate change and its impacts
Human Vulnerability and Impacts on Disadvantaged Communities	Goal 3. Ensure healthy lives and promote well-being for all at all ages Goal 4. Ensure inclusive and equitable quality education and promote lifelong learning opportunities for all Goal 5. Achieve gender equality and empower all women and girls Goal 8. Promote sustained, inclusive and sustainable economic growth, full and productive employment and decent work for all Goal 10. Reduce inequality within and among countries Goal 16. Promote peaceful and inclusive societies for sustainable development, provide access to justice for all and build effective, accountable and inclusive institutions at all levels
Infrastructure Change	Goal 6. Ensure the availability and sustainable management of water and sanitation for all
Land Use Change and the Growing Eco	Goal 12. Ensure sustainable consumption and production patterns

| Footprint | Goal 14. Conserve and sustainably use the oceans, seas and marine resources for sustainable development |
| | Goal 15. Protect, restore and promote sustainable use of terrestrial ecosystems, sustainably manage forests, combat desertification, and halt and reverse land degradation and halt biodiversity loss |

Resilient and Sustainable Cities

As discussed in Chapter 4, resilience and sustainability are now clearly linked. Government is clearly focused on protecting infrastructure. In the business world the concept of resilience has grown significantly.

My colleague Joseph Fiksel, in his book "Resilient by Design" describes how businesses are grappling with the challenges of climate change and volatility in a hyper-connected, global economy. He notes that they are paying increasing attention to their organization's resilience—the capacity to survive, adapt, and flourish in the face of turbulent change. Sudden natural disasters and unforeseen supply chain disruptions are increasingly common in the new normal. Pursuing business as usual is no longer viable, and many companies are unaware of how fragile they really are.

To cope with these challenges, management needs a new paradigm that takes an integrated view of the built environment, ecosystems, and the social fabric in which their businesses operate. Fiksel argues that instead of merely reacting to disruptions, companies can become more resilient through the purposeful design of their facilities, supply chains, and business practices. The book provides case studies of organizations that are designing resilience into their business processes and explains how to connect with important external systems—stakeholders, communities, infrastructure, supply chains, and natural resources—and create innovative, dynamic organizations that survive and prosper under any circumstances.

For EPA, a robust and resilient economy and the protection of health and the environment are all components of a sustainable society.

Business-Government Cooperation

The combined pressures of social, economic, and environmental impacts have inspired many business sectors to better understand and embrace the importance of sustainability. Leading executives generally accept the fact that protecting the environment reduces long-term risk, builds customer support, and makes good business sense. Many business leaders are adopting the circular economy framework and focusing on the full life cycle of production and use.

Business and government are critical players in economic and material needs, a stable society, and building a sustainable future. The World Business Council for Sustainable Development (WBCSD) has developed an ambitious agenda to assist global industries in moving toward sustainable growth. The Council's Vision 2050 report coined the phrase "green race," and outlines a "pathway that will require fundamental changes in governance structures, economic frameworks, business and human behavior." The report argues that these changes are "necessary, feasible and offer tremendous business opportunities for companies that turn sustainability into strategy."

At the same time, business and government leaders acknowledge the complexity of coupled human and natural systems, which require flexible and adaptive policies to achieve sustainable and resilient outcomes. This only accentuates the need for partnership and collaboration between federal agencies and all stakeholders.

In preparing for the 2012 Rio +20 Anniversary Summit, I worked with many business and academic colleagues to prepare a paper on "Creating the Future We Want" in which we emphasized the importance of business-government cooperation.[29]

In the paper, we noted five major trends:

1. The world is not on a sustainable path. Our current oversized footprint, augmented by continuing economic and population growth, will result in increasing pressures on energy, water, land, and food, which in turn stress both government and business.
2. Global megatrends are driving science, innovation, and new business models that can help solve present and future problems, but existing innovative approaches and business models must be scaled up.

---

[29] Alan D. Hecht, Joseph Fiksel, Scott C. Fulton, Terry F. Yosie, Neil C. Hawkins, Heinz Leuenberger, Jay Golden, and Thomas E. Lovejoy, "Creating the Future We Want, *SSPP*, V 8, Issue 2: 2-12.

3. Several emerging frameworks—good governance based on the rule of law, the green economy, shared values, and stewardship—present opportunities for accelerated progress in sustainability. These frameworks must be better understood, integrated, and disseminated globally.
4. The positive linkages among economic growth, social well-being, and environmental protection are not yet fully appreciated or understood. Further research and education are clearly needed.
5. New collaborations are needed among business, government, academia, and NGOs.

We did note that major advances in science and technology and in business practices are promoting innovation and sustainable solutions, although more needs to be done. Hence, we firmly believe that global sustainability can be realized through effective business and government collaborations.

EPA at 50 in 2020

We now come to the end of this book. After all I have shown, are you optimistic or pessimistic about the future? Can the federal government and Congress converge on sound environment and economic policies? Can governments around the world work together to achieve a safer and more sustainable future? Can we deal with abating future climate change?

The politics going on today, especially related to the EPA raises serious concerns about the future. What will EPA be like on its 50th Birthday in 2020? Activities of the Trump Administration are largely focused on EPA's classic role as the regulator of clean air and water and the protection of human health. Unfortunately, it is doing so while decreasing the EPA budget and staff.

While EPA always focuses on health and the environment, it has evolved over nearly 50 years to see things in a more integrated manner and aims to develop tools and approaches to achieve a resilient and sustainable society. What is needed today is what former Administrator Jackson said on EPA's 40th birthday:

> "As we celebrate 40 years of incredible accomplishments, we find ourselves at a critical juncture. We have a **new awareness of environmental complexity** and, at the same time, we have new tools, insights, and experiences to guide our mission. It **is time to rise to the**

challenges of today, using the best of what we have, to meet the needs of the current generation while preserving the ability of future generations to meet theirs as well."

For Business and government there are clearly 7 critical questions, conceived by my colleague Joseph Fiksel and I, to ask in achieving a resilient and sustainable society.

Sustainability Questions	Resilience Questions
1. Will the action protect human health and the environment? Will it integrate and optimize environmental, economic, and social benefits? 2. Will the action conserve natural resources—energy, water, materials, land, ecosystems, and air—through prudent use/reuse, protection, and/or restoration? 3. Does the action reflect an orientation toward life cycle, multimedia, pollution prevention, minimizing wastes and toxics, and advancing multiple goals through systems thinking? 4. Does the action consider the full diversity of available policy and program tools to stimulate and reinforce sustainable outcomes, innovating and collaborating wherever necessary? 5. Will the action improve people's lives, creating better and healthier communities rather than just correcting problems? Does it consider vulnerable populations (e.g., children and the elderly) who may bear disproportionate burdens?	1. Does the action reflect the full spectrum of risks and disruptive forces that may affect both human and natural well-being? 2. Does the action recognize the interdependence of the built environment, infrastructure, and the environment, including the potential for cascading failures? 3. Will the action help to reduce the exposure and vulnerability of critical industrial and ecological assets to extreme events, such as natural disasters or catastrophic failures? 4. Does the action tend to increase the inherent robustness, reliability, flexibility, agility, and/or effectiveness of existing economic and social activities, even for unforeseen threats? 5. Does the action result from considering a diverse portfolio of resilience capabilities available from both public and private organizations that share common goals? 6. Does the action seek to strengthen the resilience of existing systems by learning from prior disruptions and

6. Does the action identify meaningful sustainability outcomes and include appropriate metrics? Are there plans to track progress, learn from experience, innovate, and adapt? 7. Does the action include plans to share as much information as possible and engage everyone to take active responsibility for achieving sustainable outcomes?	adapting, rather than simply returning to "normal" operation? 7. Will the action identify leading indicators of potential disruptions, keep track of external forces and trends, and identify new scenarios that may create future challenges?

Addressing the problems of the 21st century will require a combination of strategies, including the creative use of existing environmental policies and regulations, innovative application of science and technology, and collaboration among stakeholders.

The experiences of seeing the past, living today, and projecting the future make it urgent that we put politics aside and act to protect the health and security of our people. This is why I have advanced actions to build a resilient and sustainable society.

As I noted in the introduction, the next steps forward are to:

1. Advance and apply science, technology, and innovation.
2. Build smarter business practices that promote sustainable solutions.
3. Coordinate activities across international organizations, nations, regional and local governments, and NGOs.
4. Develop more effective collaboration between business and government.
5. Enhance public understanding and support of sustainability.

6. Foster collaboration between political organizations.

Let's hope the present and all future Administrations can do this to achieve a green and safe society.